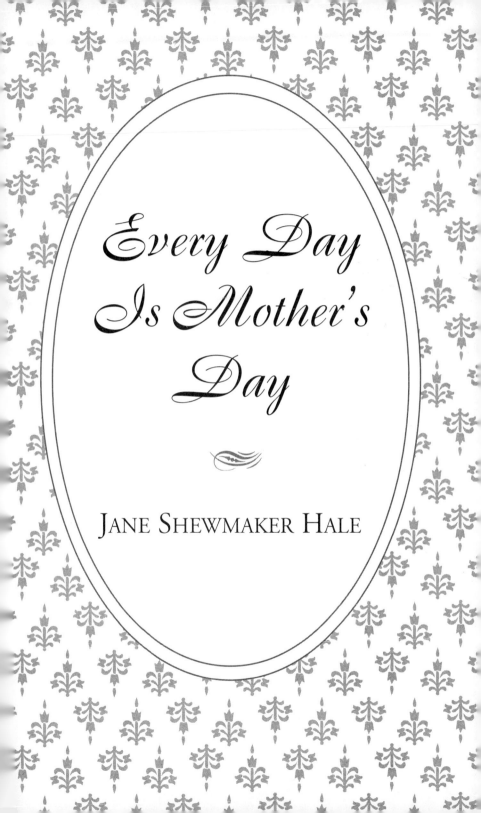

Every Day Is Mother's Day

JANE SHEWMAKER HALE

This book is for you!

_____ _____
                                    Date

From _____

This gift is my way of saying "I love you,"
It's filled with laughter and a tear or two;
"Hand me down" stories filled with family remind me of you,
Hope it reminds you of me.

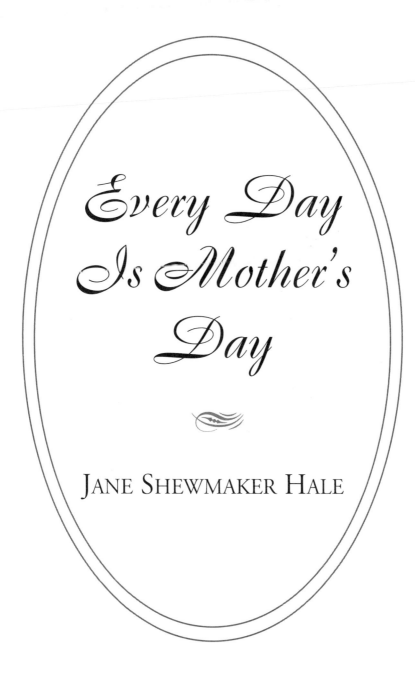

Every Day Is Mother's Day

JANE SHEWMAKER HALE

Skyward Publishing, Inc.
Dallas, Texas
www.skywardpublishing.com

© Copyright 2003 by Skyward Publishing, Inc.

Publisher: Skyward Publishing, Inc.
              Dallas, Texas

Cover artist: *Dick Johns*

Library of Congress Cataloging-in-Publication Data

Hale, Jane Shewmaker, 1934-
   Every day is Mother's Day / by Jane Shewmaker Hale.
      p. cm.
   ISBN 1-881554-32-5
1. Mothers. 2. Mother and child. 3. Grandmothers. 4. Grandparent and child. I. Title
HQ759.H1864 2003   306.874'3--dc21
                                        2003000524

Printed in the United States of America

DEDICATION

*I*n memory of my mom, Dorothy Inez Sadler Shewmaker

And, for her sisters, Aunt Ree, Aunt Ella, Aunt Molly, my image-Aunt Joyce, and their only brother, Uncle Don. They made those long ago summer days so sweet.

CONTENTS

CONTENTS

SECTION III
Traditions: FAMILY FOLKLORE

CONTENTS

Section VII
Sincerely

ACKNOWLEDGMENTS

*T*hanks, Mom, for being our link to generations of mothers before you. Can we ever say "Thanks" enough for mothers like you?

Thanks to your mother, whom we called Mamie, for teaching us to express our love with hugs and kisses.

Thanks, Mom, for being the cornerstone of our family of four: my dad, Blaine; my brother, Rex; me, Jane; and, of course, you.

Thanks, Mom, for being a mother to our spouses—my husband, Bob, and Rex's wife, Joan.

Thanks, Mom, for spoiling our children—your grandchildren—Ricky, Reggie, Mitchell, and Lucas Hale, and Tom, Joey, Sharon, Connie, and Terry Shewmaker.

Thanks, Mom, for giving new meaning to the title *Great*-grandma or your special name, "Gobbies."

THE HALES

Rick and Karen: Blaine, Nathan, and Zachary
Reggie and Gai: Chase, Cali, and Colby
Mitch and Suzyn: Nicholas, Chayla, and Austin
Lucas: Jacob

THE SHEWMAKERS

Tom and Barbara: Brian, Amy, and Cortney
Joey and Jeni: Jason, Jana, and Jordan
Sharon and Kelly: Taira, Matt, and Chelsey
Terry and Christie: Ryan, Kayla, and Dusty
Connie and Matt: Emily

KNOWING SOMEONE CARES

The young couple was expecting its second child in August. It was a hot summer and the mother-to-be soon filled out her clothes to capacity. Bending to do her daily chores while tending a two-year-old son was difficult. Donning men's overalls gave her the room she needed to move around more freely.

This may be an accepted fashion now, but in 1934 women who were expecting were considered unsightly. The recommended prescription for at least five of the nine months of pregnancy was stay at home. The young mother wearing overalls was probably considered flaunting fashion.

It was a long hot summer of pregnancy for the woman who was to become my mother on August 28, 1934. Perhaps the freedom of movement I experienced as I grew my first nine months was a forerunner for the freedom of expression Mom taught me as I grew up.

My mom wowed, or impressed greatly, her image on my life. Daily she taught my brother, Rex, and me the importance of giving our best to any situation. Honesty, truthfulness, dignity, and love ranked high on her list, along with commitment and achievement.

Mom was a career mother. Every day was Mother's Day for Mom. Family was her priority. Being chairman of the family board (or paddle), she used her position as a physical reminder to keep us on the right path. "This hurts me more than it does you" were words I didn't understand until I walked in her shoes.

By the time I was a mother, she was a grandmother who taught me another lesson with these words, "Grandkids are great! You can spoil them all you want and then send them home!"

By the time I learned these words were true, Mom was a great-grandmother who shared these words with her children, grandchildren, and great-grandchildren when they'd give her a hug and kiss. She'd say, "That's what keeps me going—knowing someone cares!"

FOREWORD

I endorse the dedicated efforts of *Every Day Is Mother's Day* by Jane Hale as a workable tool for inspiration to all mothers.

PEGGY VINING

*A*ll that I am and ever hope to be I owe to my dear mother. I quote President Abe Lincoln to echo my feelings about my own mother, Winnie Caudle, who during her lifetime was the epitome of all a mother should be: loving, caring, nurturing, understanding, God-fearing, and unselfish, always putting her family before herself.

My husband, Don, and I have been married almost fifty-four years. God has blessed our union with five children. We have eleven grandchildren and are looking forward to the arrival of a great-grandson.

My mother was my mentor and source of inspiration as I reared my family. A mother is a child's first teacher, first model of behavior, and first knowledge of God. I am confident that "the hands that rock the cradle rule the world," not by power but through love, dedication, devotion, and determination.

I have been a nurturer of children my entire life, it seems. My sister was my eleventh birthday present. She was my "baby doll." My love of teaching had it roots at this early age. For thirty-two years, my career as a teacher touched over six thousand children in both public and private schools. Twenty-one of those years I was Instructor/Director of the UALR Children's Center, a laboratory school for the University of Arkansas at Little Rock. During those years I began to see the demise of the family unit as I had known it. I felt that too many expectations had been lowered, and it saddened me to realize that family values, morals, and manners were beginning to be diminished. My heart goes out to the families who are trying so hard to balance the "needs" and the "positions" society seems to require of them.

As a mother my greatest surprise and honor was being named 1982 Arkansas Mother of the Year." My award was presented at the state capitol by former President Bill Clinton, then Governor of Arkansas. It was my awesome privilege to represent the mothers of Arkansas at the American Mothers, Inc. Convention in Utah. AMI is headquartered in Washington, D.C. The purpose of the organization is to "foster the moral and spiritual foundation of the home." For sixty-eight years this organization has assisted families in making the world a better place for children.

I have worked in AMI since 1982, twelve years as state president and on the national board for the past eight years, working in various positions because I believe that motherhood is God's gift to honor a woman and the honor should not be taken lightly.

Enjoy the job! God bless mothers!

MORE ABOUT PEGGY VINING

Peggy Vining is a resident of Little Rock, Arkansas.

She has received a "Point of Light Award" from former President George Bush for her volunteer work with the cancer society. (Peggy is a twenty-six year survivor of cancer.)

Peggy's life is dedicated to God and service to others.

She has been twice nominated for the "Top One Hundred Women in Arkansas."

She is an author and poet with seventy-five published poems.

Was Literary Chairman for Arkansas State Festival of Arts for thirteen years.

Currently President of Poets Roundtable of Arkansas (twice previously).

Director of Ozark Creative Writers Convention twelve years (on official board 30 years).

Director of Arkansas Writers Conference two years (on board over 25 years).

Past President of Arkansas Songwriters (12 years).

The Greatest Mom Award

A Mother's Day Poem just for you!

"M" is for <u>the many hugs you give me!</u>
"O" is for <u>overlooking my messes</u>.
"T" is for <u>teaching me about Jesus</u>.
"H" is for <u>helping me become independent</u>.
"E" is for <u>everything you do for me</u>.
"R" is for <u>remembering how much I love you</u>!

Put them all together, they spell mother.
Someone who means so much to me.

From: <u>Kathy</u>

Written by Kathy Hale Delone, Peggy's second daughter, at age 13.

INTRODUCTION

M-O-T-H-E-R-S

*O*riginally *Every Day Is Mother's Day* was set up to have six sections with each letter of the word M-O-T-H-E-R becoming a section heading beginning with that letter:

*M*ilestones
*O*fferings
*T*raditions
*H*ome
*E*xpressions
*R*ecollections

I added S on the end of MOTHER because I wanted this book to belong to every mother. S became Sincerely.

Sincerely is a logical way to end the book with notes from the author. You'll also find a surprise in this section. Just think of it as dessert after your meal. Mom taught me you have to finish your meal before you get to dessert.

Enjoy! And don't peek!

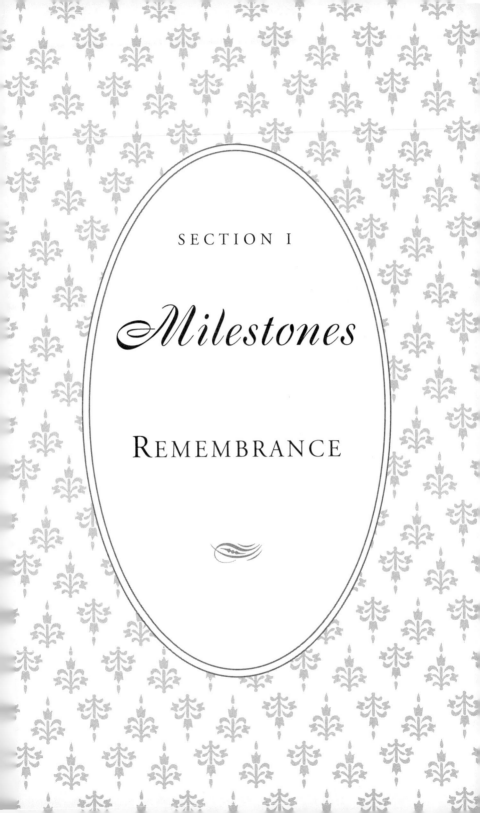

SECTION I

Milestones

REMEMBRANCE

~ *When curls were in style,*
and skirts were short, and
copying Shirley was in
for Mother. ~

I'm Not Shirley . . .
My Name Is Jane

My mother was one of many mothers who envisioned her little darling as Shirley Temple.

Growing up during the forties was a time when a lot of little girls ran the risk of losing their identities to that pretty little miss with fat curls.

Let me tell you, those curls did not come easy. Mom bade me sit atop a stool so she could arrange my hair into thick finger curls.

I obeyed, but my thoughts were outside where my brother and his gang were playing games. If I whined, "Why don't you just comb my hair out straight?" Mom would give me a *nice little girls don't talk to their mothers that way* look and say, "If you don't want me to fix your hair, I bet the little girl across the street would like to have Shirley Temple curls."

I'd give her a Shirley Temple smile as I thought, *I wish that little girl across the street was sitting here and I was next batter up!*

Anything my mom thought was a good thing for her daughter to do was surely something Shirley Temple did. From "The Good Ship Lollipop" to whatever song Shirley was singing and skipping to in her latest movie, I was subject to learn a new speech to perform for bored relatives.

I must admit my memory benefited from Mom's recitations, and my recall is something Shirley and I must surely share today.

Mom's fingers fashioned outfits that put Shirley Temple's

23

wardrobe people to shame. Alas, the one thing our clothes had in common was short skirts. Since my dresses barely covered my underpants, Mom instructed me in the art of not bending over but using my knees to go up and down. When sitting, my legs must be crossed ladylike at the ankles.

One day I flounced home from school and announced, "I'm not going to wear those short skirts to school anymore. The kids are laughing at me."

Mom gave me her guilt-trip look and said, "If Shirley Temple's mom worked her fingers to the bone to make her beautiful clothes, I bet that little saint would never say she didn't want to wear them." She then asked, "You're sure you don't want to wear your pretty little dresses to school?"

I hung on to her question for dear life, forgetting the guilt she was laying on as a warning.

"Nope, I don't want to wear short skirts."

The next morning Mom laid out a dress for me I had never seen before. Knowing she must have sewed into the night, I felt like a thankless daughter.

When I put it on, I didn't have to worry about having a dress that was too short—this one came to my ankles. I asked, "Mom, did you forget to hem this dress?"

Mom gave me her *remember, you asked for this* look and said, "Is it long enough for you? Of course, Shirley Temple would never wear a dress this long, but far be it for me to have kids laugh at my daughter because her dress is too short."

I looked up to see her smiling at me with a knowing look in her eye that seemed to say, *So, do you want to wear this or your cute little Shirley Temple dresses?*

I knew perfect little Shirley Temple would never pick up her books and stalk out in that long dress to go to school and have the kids laugh harder. But I did! I wore long dresses until my mom compromised with a suitable length for a fifth grader who leaned over at the plate when she assumed her stance to bat.

When I slid into base with a longer skirt to cover me, I'd think, *Eat your heart out, Shirley!*

I'm sure millions of little girls wanted to be "Little Shirley Temple," but as for me, I just wanted people to know . . . I'm not Shirley . . . my name is JANE!

It wasn't until years later that I discovered Shirley's middle name was Jane!

I bet Mom knew it all along. ⌢

~*When sisters were brave, and brothers were clever, and strangers were no challenge for Mother.*~

STRANGERS IN THE HOUSE

Mom left a bucket of water with a dipper in it on the back porch adjoining our bedrooms. On hot summer nights, with not even a fan to stir the breeze and air conditioning somewhere in the future, a cold drink of water was one of the most important things in our lives.

The screened-in porch ran the length of the back of the house, but the water was at the other end of the porch, just off the kitchen. If Rex and I woke and were thirsty, we'd run the length of the dark porch, grab the dipper, wet our whistles, and run back to bed.

Evenings, Mom would usually pop a huge bowl of popcorn and we'd tune in to the radio, which was our most exciting form of entertainment. Together, as a family, we'd listen to comedies like *Amos and Andy* or westerns like *The Lone Ranger*. Sometimes, we'd listen to my favorite mystery, *The Squeaky Door*.

Mom didn't like for us to listen to *The Squeaky Door* because she was afraid it would give us nightmares.

Sure enough, when we woke thirsty after listening to *The Squeaky Door*, that dark porch would be pretty scary.

If Rex woke thirsty, he'd wake me. He'd ask if I wanted a drink. I always did. I'd run with him down the porch to the pail of water. He'd grab the dipper, gulp, and dash back to bed while I was still trying to remind him Mom had told us we weren't supposed to drink from the dipper.

Mom kept every door in the house locked and the screens latched. We were completely safe. But the Man in the Moon bewitched me as he directed his own spooky show on our screened-in porch and the backyard in the wee hours of the morning.

Moonbeams filtered through the screen, outlining clothes hanging on Mom's inside line. The wind arrived on cue, breathing life into the clothes, and they became strangers swaggering about our porch.

Mom had warned me about strangers, and I had tarried too long. I longed to hurry to the safety of my bedroom, but strangers swayed dangerously close and froze me at the wrong end of the porch.

In the words of the Lone Ranger's sidekick, Tonto, "Kemo Sabe, you are cut off at the pass."

Maybe if I whispered loudly, Rex would hear me and come back. He never did. He thought I was fearless, else, why would he have wakened me in the first place? It was up to me to save myself.

Illusions of childhood came to my rescue. I closed my eyes tight and held my breath. I imagined I was invisible. Then I flattened my body against the wooden wall of the porch and edged to the safety of the bedroom wing. Once there, I opened my eyes, breathed deeply, and casually strolled into bed—in case anyone was awake to notice.

They never were. I could hear Rex's steady breathing approaching an imitation of Dad's full-fledged snore. Mom's soft breathing mocked her restless slumber. They would never know the perils of our porch.

One night when Rex woke me to ask if I were thirsty, I wasn't. But he kept on asking until I began to believe I was. I got up and he headed out, looking back to be sure I was following. It occurred to me he knew of the danger lurking on our back porch and might be frightened too. I stopped in my tracks!

Rex was at the dipper, gulping, as I slipped back toward the bedroom and into my bed.

I heard a loud whisper from the other end of the porch.

I wasn't about to return to that porch if it were dangerous enough to scare my big brother. I closed my eyes tight! Waiting!

Imagination is a wonderful thing. The strangers lurking in the shadows of our porch moved into the corners of my mind. My brother was in their clutches! I had left him alone!

Mom's remembered words, "You kids look after each other when I can't do the job for you," caused me to jump up and start toward the porch. I heard a sound! Scrape, rattle, heavy breathing. Oh! No! The strangers had my brother and they were coming after me.

I looked toward my parents' bedroom. Surely Dad's snore was terrible enough to ward off any danger. Maybe not! I took the coward's way out. I scrambled back into bed and pulled the covers over my head.

Footsteps were approaching! *Where are you, Lone Ranger? Tonto? If I ever needed you, I need you now!*

Strip! Yank! The covers were ripped from my grasp. Hands covered my mouth just as I opened it to yell.

"Coward! Sissy! Little cheater!" Rex hissed the words.

"Quick, Rex! The strangers are coming," I warned.

I stopped as I realized my brother was smothering laughter. He wasn't mad anymore. He was laughing at *me* as he headed to bed.

Anger was my bravest weapon against a bigger, more clever brother. I jumped up and headed to his bed, ready to do battle for all the nights he'd left me alone at the other end of the porch.

I heard a soft snore as Rex drifted off to dreamland.

I was the only one awake, again. Me and the strangers!

"Silly! Sissy! Coward!" I repeated my brother's words.

"Jane! Rex! Are you kids up?" Mom's voice carried softly, sternly, over the roar of Dad's sleep.

Rex stirred. "Jane wanted a drink."

"I did not! Rex . . ."

"That's enough! You kids get to sleep, before I . . ." Mom's voice stilled us and the strangers. The clothes on her back porch line hung in the moonlight drying, just as she'd left them.

I crawled into bed, confident Mom would take care of any strangers that passed my way. She always did. ⌒

When resolutions were devout,
intentions were strong, and
commitment was vital
for Mother.

NEW YEAR'S RESOLUTIONS

*M*om called to Mr. and Mrs. Russell, "Happy New Year."
They returned her greeting.

Mom waved goodbye to Rex and me as we walked
up the sidewalk with our neighbors who took us to Sunday school
each week. I knew we wouldn't be out of sight before she would be
cleaning and cooking to get our Sunday family dinner ready. Sending
her children off to church scrubbed, shined, with Bible and offering
in hand, was Mom's contribution to religion at that time in her life.

"You be good and listen to everything so you can tell me about it
when you get home," Mom always admonished us.

Rex and I knew if she ever got a bad report on us, we were in big
trouble. We didn't have any problems. What could you do in church
to get in trouble?

Our Sunday school teacher asked, "Have you made your New
Year's resolutions?"

I nudged the girl sitting beside me. "What's a resolution?"

She whispered, "It's a promise you make in January. You're supposed to keep it all year. Good luck!"

Our teacher saw us whispering and asked if we'd stand and give
our resolution.

My friend went first. "I resolve to say my prayers every night, do
my homework, and help my parents."

My mind was working overtime. New Year's resolutions are so
neat! Kind of like making promises, or little prayers, for a better self.

On the table in front of me were my Bible, my scripture book, and my little purse.

Our teacher cleared her throat. "Jane?"

I stood up, swallowed hard, and began, "I resolve to read my Bible every day so I'll have my scripture readings every Sunday." I looked down and rediscovered my purse. "Oh, yes! And to tithe, that is, give ten percent to the Lord."

"I look forward to the results of your resolutions." Our teacher smiled.

I could hardly wait to get home and tell my family about New Year's resolutions.

Mom was in the kitchen trying to take up the last of the fried chicken, pull the biscuits from the oven, stir the gravy, and scowl at Dad, who had the Sunday paper spread across the table.

A plume of smoke drifted from Dad's mouth as he balanced himself precariously on the back two legs of his chair.

"At Sunday school we learned about New Year's resolutions. Have you made your resolutions yet?" I asked.

Dad laid down the comic section. "I resolve to help the Democrats get re-elected, help Al Capp write a better cartoon, and stuff myself with chicken if your mom ever gets it on the table." He chuckled.

I giggled until I happened to look at Mom. Dad had completely missed the look she gave him as he stubbed out his cigar in her best saucer. It was just as well—I knew that look.

"Mom," I asked hesitantly, "what about you?"

"Jane, why don't you put the butter and preserves on the table— if you can find room." Mom glanced purposely at Dad's newspaper.

Rex scooted into his chair, looking impatiently toward our back porch where several boys had gathered for their regular Sunday afternoon basketball game.

Mom stood by the table, holding the platter of fried chicken. Dad looked up, grinned, and reached for his fork.

Oh, Dad, don't make that mistake, I prayed.

Mom returned the platter of chicken to the stove. "Jane, help your dad clean up his Sunday paper. Now there's some good resolution material." The tone of her voice set Dad in motion.

Mom walked to the back porch, picked up the basketball, and tossed it to one of the boys. "Rex will be out after he's finished with dinner."

The door slammed and the sound of a bouncing basketball echoed in the silence of our kitchen.

"Mom, can I help you do anything else?" I could think of a dozen resolutions: one of them was *not to slam the back door!*

Mom nodded for me to be seated. She returned the platter of chicken to the cleared table and seated herself.

I broke the silence. "I resolved to read my Bible every day so I'll know my scripture verses. And . . . I promised to tithe—give ten percent of my allowance each week to Sunday school."

Rex's head was tilted toward the sound of the basketball game. "God should get rich off that."

Dad reached for his fork.

Mom silenced him and Rex with a look. "Perhaps you'd like to say grace, Jane."

I had reached for my fork and was eyeing a piece of white meat—the same piece Rex was eyeballing.

Silence reigned!

I knew the prayer my dad would say: "Good bread, good meat, good GOD, let's eat." I glanced at Mom and knew I didn't dare. I searched my mind for the prayer my teacher had closed our lesson with this morning.

"Thank you, God, for this class, er, family. Thank you for the new year. Help us to be better people and resolve to give you all the praise. Amen."

Rex forked my piece of white meat. Dad got the other piece. The biscuits started around the table, followed by the gravy.

After lunch, Rex ran for the backyard. I looked after him longingly. I usually got to play basketball if there weren't enough boys. I stood up and started to clear the table.

"You go on, Jane. I think your dad wants to help me."

Surprised, I looked at Dad.

He nodded. Maybe he was starting his list of resolutions already.

I didn't wait for them to change their minds. From the back porch, I yelled, "Mom, you never told me your resolutions."

Mom laughed. "Oh! I think I'll just help your dad make a few. Let's see, we could start with not reading the paper at the table, not smoking around the children, and if he breaks the legs on my kitchen chairs from bending backward in them, he'll buy me a new dining room set."

Dad chuckled. "Like my old pappy always said, New Year's resolutions are make to be broken."

I slammed the back door and stopped short. Dad's old pappy was right! I'd already broken one of my New Year's resolutions. I hoped Mom wasn't listening. ⌇

~ When ideas were whimsy,
notions were weird, and
explanations were chores
for Mother. ~

MOTHER'S WEIRD AND CRAZY NOTIONS

When I was small, Mom said I must have thought my mouth was for filling with whatever I had in my hands at the time: food, a pencil, paper, my handkerchief, and even coins. She scolded me each time she saw an unacceptable object enter my mouth. "Jane, get that coin out of your mouth. You don't know where it's been. It could have been on a *dead man's eye.*"

I almost swallowed the coin. The idea that it had been on a dead man's eye and now rested in my mouth left me sputtering. Out came the coin.

Mother's Weird and Crazy Notions Book was full of cautions, but that was one bit of advice I remembered. Being an inquisitive little girl, I wanted more information. I learned when people died, sometimes coins were placed on their eyes to keep the lids closed until they were prepared for burial. Mom was right. That coin might have been on a dead man's eye!

I had nightmares for months afterwards, especially when I stayed up late and ate junk food before retiring. In my dreams, I'd walk into a room where a man was laid out on a slab (just like in the movies) to be prepared for his funeral. He'd have coins on his eyes.

Mouth gaping, I'd lean over to see if the coins were pennies, nickels, or perhaps quarters. Sure enough, the dead man's eyes popped open and the coins flew right into my open mouth.

I'd wake up screaming and run to get in bed with my parents. As I cuddled close, I babbled about dead men with coins on their eyes and in my mouth.

Mom would say, "I knew you shouldn't have eaten all that greasy popcorn. Tomorrow night you'll go to bed earlier. Remember what your dad says, 'Early to bed and early to rise makes a man healthy, wealthy, and wise . . . and not have bad dreams.'" She promptly rolled over and went to sleep.

I lay there trying to make the connection. If I went to bed early, I might be healthy because I'd get more sleep. That could make me wiser. The wealthy part didn't make sense. Perhaps, if I could snatch coins from the dead man's eyes in my dreams, I could save up and become wealthy.

On that thought, I went to sleep to have the same nightmare. I had forgotten each time I leaned toward the dead man, his eyes opened. If he were ready for burial and didn't need his coins, it seemed all right to take them. But if he were still alive, taking the coins was stealing.

I had learned whistling helped soothe me when I was afraid. So, I lay in the dark, snug against Mom's back, and whistled softly. Darkness magnified sound. I heard Mom's soft breathing and Dad's snore. It was Dad's snore that caught my attention. His intake of breath was the snore sound, and the sound coming out turned into a whistle. So I tried to match my whistle with his and soon we were harmonizing.

Until . . ."Who's whistling?" Dad's voice boomed.

I stopped whistling, suddenly conscious I was doing a solo.

"Hush, you're snoring," Mom said to Dad. She turned and cuddled me against her.

Soon Dad was asleep and whistling his own solo.

Mom whispered in my ear, "A whistling woman and a crowing hen always come to some bad end."

Before I could question her, Mom's soft breathing told me she had gone to sleep.

Why did women who whistled come to a bad end and not men? I shifted to the second part of Mom's warning and . . .

"Cock-a-doodle-do!"

I sat up in Mom and Dad's bed. I was alone. *What am I doing here?* I wondered.

"Cock-a-doodle-do!"

I got up and padded toward the back porch. As I passed Rex's bed, I heard the crowing again.

"Stupid animal, don't you know a crowing hen always comes to some bad end?"

Rex roused from sleep. "That's not a hen crowing—it's a rooster. Hens don't crow."

It dawned on me a hen was a woman chicken. So, if a whistling woman and a crowing woman hen always came to some bad end, what about men and roosters?

Mom's voice sounded from the kitchen, "Jane, are you and Rex up? Breakfast is ready. Get up and get dressed and be sure and put on clean underwear because . . ."

Rex and I looked at each other and laughed as we finished Mom's sentence, "You never know when you might be in a car wreck." ⌒

*~When customs prevailed, and
eavesdropping was rude, and
discipline was a decision
for Mother. ~*

MISTER G. H.

*O*ver the clatter of dishes in the kitchen, Mom remarked, "Well, it finally looks like we're going to get some sunshine."
Dad replied, "You might know February 2 would be clear. If I can see my shadow, you can bet old G. H. will see his."

I heard the scrape of a chair as Dad rose from the table. I could visualize his dragging his jacket from the back of the chair. Then I heard shuffling footsteps and giggles.

A melody drifted into our bedroom as Dad crooned, "Button up your overcoat when the wind is free. Take good care of yourself, you belong to me." I knew he was swinging Mom about the room in a jig.

"Be still, Blaine. We'll wake the kids."

A long silence usually meant a smooch.

Then, the closing of the back door usually meant, See ya, when I see ya.

"Who's old G. H.?" I wondered aloud.

"Groundhog. Shut up, go to sleep," Rex mumbled.

February 2—groundhog—shadow. The puzzle pieces wouldn't fit. Cautiously I eased out of bed and padded in the direction of the kitchen.

Mom looked up in surprise. "Are you sick?"

"No, Mom."

I sat down at the table and picked up a piece of bacon. I wanted to ask about old G. H., but I'd been warned about eavesdropping.

Mom looked out the kitchen window with an eye to the clothesline poles. "Looks like old Mister Sunshine is going to visit us today."

What about old G. H.?

Carefully, I phrased my question. "Do you think winter is ever going to be over?"

"According to the expert, your father, we'll have about six more weeks of it." She hummed as she cleaned the remains of breakfast.

"How does Dad know?"

"Today is February 2. Your dad believes when the groundhog wakes up, if he sees his shadow, he'll go back in his hole and we'll have six more weeks of winter."

Rex was right. Old G. H. was the groundhog.

"What does a groundhog look like?" I was drawing a mental image of the hog lot on my grandpa's farm.

"Umm, I'm not sure."

"How does he know to wake up February 2? Does he have an alarm clock?"

Mom smiled. "Ask your dad—that'll be a good question for him."

At school, we learned that people from Germany and Great Britain brought the custom of the groundhog, or woodchuck, and his shadow to America. Dad was right!

"Science has not confirmed this," Miss Johnson stated, "and, class . . . no one goes out at recess."

We looked toward the windows where rain splashed against the panes. Clouds claimed the sky.

By the time school was over, the sun was out again. I splashed through puddles heading for home. I wondered—was winter over, or not? I would find out from the expert at dinner.

"Dad, did you see old G. H. today?"

Dad looked at Mom.

She shrugged.

"Who's old G. H.?" Dad asked.

"You know, Dad, this morning you told Mom if you could see

your shadow, old G. H. could see his." I stopped!

Mom and Dad exchanged glances, which spelled out *eavesdropping*.

I hurried on, "Our teacher told us the groundhog legend. You know, about waking up on February 2 and all. Dad, Mom said to ask you if the groundhog had an alarm clock to wake him February 2."

Dad threw back his head and roared with laughter.

Oh, boy! I thought. When Dad was in a good mood, things went a lot easier.

"Do you think he saw it, Jane?"

"Depends on what time of the day he crawled out to look."

After dinner Mom cleared her throat, catching Dad's attention, and glanced in my direction. I knew I was in trouble.

"Jane, help your mother with the dishes and go to bed early."

I pouted up at Dad. He knew this was the night my favorite scary program, *The Squeaky Door*, was on the radio.

He swatted my behind, playfully, and leaned down to whisper in his same-old, same-old logic in my ear, "Early to bed and early to rise, makes you healthy, wealthy, wise . . . and not an eavesdropper."

That night I lay in bed, missing my radio program.

Mom came in to check on me. She smoothed my covers, and just as she pressed her lips against my cheek for a good night kiss, commercial time came on the radio in the next room.

The announcer spoke loud and clear, so even I could hear, "Happy February 2! It's Groundhog Day. Looks like we'll have another six weeks of winter in New York. The sun was out all day. That bugger must have seen his shadow."

My mind shifted into gear. If old G. H. saw his shadow in New York, but not here, would we both have six weeks of winter?

In the other room, Rex spoke up. "I bet if Jane heard that she'd be wondering how the groundhog could predict winter if the weather was different all over the world."

They laughed.

"Did you hear that, Jane? I wondered about that too," Mom

whispered.

"Hear what, Mom?" I asked.

Far be it from me to ask. I didn't even hear it. I never eavesdrop.

Mom cleared her throat the way she did just before she laughed. A smile settled over her lips.

Just before I went to sleep, I reached up and hugged Mom. I gave her a kiss. Being a kid was hard, but I bet being a mom wasn't an easy job either. ⁓

⌒When home was love, and
blessings were shared, and
heartache was a question
for Mother.⌒

TURK

I guess Mom thought 4-H would be a good place for me to spend some of my time one summer. Most of the kids were from surrounding country schools. A few lived in town as I did. I met Alberta at a 4-H meeting the summer before I entered fourth grade in 1943.

"Mom, all the kids have animals in 4-H. What will I tell my teacher when she asks me if I have animals?"

"Tell her you've got a dog and some chickens."

"But Spot belongs to Dad. The chickens are yours."

"In this family we share. Spot and my chickens belong to all of us."

Mom raised *battery* chickens. Battery chickens have a short life. When they were ready to eat, Mom killed them, cleaned them, and sold them to people in town for fryers. Rex and I had learned not to get attached to the chickens. Rex said those chickens were good soldiers who gave their lives for someone's Sunday dinner. Dad said our country was in the middle of World War II, and Rex labeled our chickens patriotic.

In 4-H we visited some of the farms where our members lived. I saw watermelons growing and got a taste of one directly from the vine. We visited farms with cows, hogs, chickens, and geese. I volunteered my grandparents' farm where they were baling hay.

Mom made me a sack lunch for our field trips. Everyone brought one, and we'd spread a pallet and eat together. The main sandwich was baloney, mayonnaise, and bread. A few brought an apple or a pear. Some lucky ones had a Babe Ruth, Butterfinger, or Hershey's bar. They'd share and we were all happy.

Just before school started in September, we visited Alberta's farm where her family raised turkeys. Alberta showed our group how she helped feed the turkeys. One of the turkeys followed Alberta and pecked at her hand. We thought he was trying to bite her, but Alberta told us this was Turk's way of getting her attention. She proudly introduced us to her pet turkey. Turk was almost full grown and he strutted about the turkey lot with a most important air. I'd have given anything for a pet like Turk and told Alberta so. She smiled proudly and stroked Turk's feathers.

At supper that evening, I couldn't wait to tell Mom about our day at the turkey farm.

Mom explained Alberta's family raised turkeys to sell just as she raised battery chickens, only on a bigger scale. She said, "Big turkey farms all over raise turkeys for Thanksgiving. Some of those turkeys will be shipped overseas to our fighting boys."

"Will we have turkey for Thanksgiving?" I asked.

Mom shook her head. "There's a war on, remember? We ration so our soldiers can have food to keep them strong to fight for our country."

September came and school started. 4-H still met on Saturdays.

Halloween claimed the spotlight in October. Then, November brought Thanksgiving!

Mom taught me how to draw my very own turkey. "Put your hand down on the paper, spread your fingers and thumb, trace around the whole hand, beginning with the wrist area." My thumb became the turkey's head; the spread fingers were the feathers. I drew an eye in the thumb and colored my turkey golden brown like Turk.

We had a special 4-H meeting the Saturday before Thanksgiving. I could hardly wait! Everyone was to bring a sack lunch and, for a surprise, a little bit of sugar, which was rationed because of the war. Mom also put in a little bottle of red sprinkles to give to my group leader.

"Mom, I hope Alberta is there. She's been absent the last two 4-H meetings. I hope nothing's happened to her or Turk."

Mom said, "It's probably a busy time on their farm with Thanksgiving and turkey time coming up fast." She stopped as though considering and put in another bottle of purple sprinkles. "Jane, give these to the teacher for Alberta. It may be a sad time for her."

Alberta was there! Mom was right! But, how could she have known Alberta would be sad? My friend sat by herself and wouldn't talk to anyone.

Our group leader asked how many of us had remembered our sugar. We raised our hands. Several others had bottles of sprinkles the same as Mom had sent with me.

I announced loudly so Alberta could hear, "Mom sent this bottle of purple sprinkles for Alberta. Shall I give them to her or to you?"

The leader smiled. "Did you hear that, Alberta? Your friend brought purple sprinkles for your sugar cookies."

But Alberta didn't look up. I'd never seen her so sad.

That morning we made sugar cookies, cut them in the shape of turkeys, and baked them in the oven for our special dessert treat.

Everyone was thrilled except Alberta. She started crying when we cut the turkey cookies and put them in the oven to bake.

When we broke for sack lunch, I scooted close to Alberta to see if I could help.

As we pulled out our baloney sandwiches, I tried to think of something that would cheer her up. "How's Turk?"

Alberta sobbed, "Turk's dead. Dad shipped him off with the rest of the turkeys for Thanksgiving two weeks ago."

I cried for Turk too. Then, I looked toward the table where the turkey cookies for dessert were waiting. Several turkeys had purple breasts. It reminded me of the purple hearts they awarded soldiers for bravery. I wondered if Mom might have known about Turk and had the same idea that was forming in my mind when she sent the purple sprinkles.

When our leader passed the cookie plate, I took two purple heart cookies and gave one to Alberta. I tried to remember what Rex had said about our chickens being good soldiers.

I told Alberta, "Turk was a good soldier. He gave his life to help make our soldier boys strong and win the war."

Alberta smiled for the first time that day.

We had talked so much we had forgotten to eat our baloney sandwiches. I had an idea. I showed Alberta how Mom had taught me to make our very own turkey. We placed our hands on our baloney sandwiches, tore around our fingers and thumb, and laughed as we had turkey for dinner.

Before the 4-H meeting broke up, our group leader asked us all to stand. "Tell what you are thankful for."

"I'm thankful for my mom and our home and family," I said.

Alberta smiled through her tears as she said, "I'm thankful to have had a pet named Turk who was a good soldier. He gave his life to help make our soldier boys strong and was awarded a purple heart."

I smiled, thinking how pleased Mom would be when I told her how her purple sprinkles had made Alberta's day happier. ∽

> ∼ *"When" was our childhood,*
> *reality is right now, and*
> *remembrance is a tribute*
> *for Mother.* ∼

"WHEN" WAS OUR CHILDHOOD

I double-dog-dare you to remember when mom, family, school, and playing games were the most important things in your life.

Mom taught me jingles and chants like this one:

"Eeny-meeny-miney-mo,
Catch a feller by the toe.
If he hollers, let him go,
Eeny-meeny-miney-mo.
My mother told me to pick the very best one.
O-u-t spells out-you-go,
You old dirty dishrag, you!"

Mom liked for my brother and me to play in our neighborhood close to home. As evening settled into twilight, we knew it wouldn't be long until we'd hear our mom's voice hollering us inside while other kids' voices in the distance were still calling, "Bob–Rio!"

We'd head inside where Mom would be waiting. She'd tell us, "I'm glad to see you enjoying this time you have together. It's the best time of your life."

Something in the wistfulness of her voice made me think she was remembering when she was a kid and played with her friends.

I asked Rex, "Do you think Mom used to play games like we do now?"

He nodded. "I think all of our friends' moms and dads have always played games. That's how the games and their rules got passed down through the years."

I lay in bed later thinking: *Someday I'll be old like Mom. I'll see my kids and grandkids playing and I'll remember when I was a kid and played games.*

Here are a few of those memories I'd like to share.

FAVORITE GAMES:
Blind man's bluff
Break the wall of China
Hide-and-seek
Hopscotch
H-O-R-S-E in basketball
Kick-the-can
Mother, may I?
Red rover
Red light, green light
Simon says
Work-up in baseball

WHAT FUN IT WAS:
Catching fireflies or lightning bugs in jars
Getting your tickle box turned over and giggling so hard you couldn't stop
Having pillow fights
Having rubber gun fights
Having water balloon fights
Picking the petals off daisies to the rhyme, "Loves-me, loves-me-not"
Playing jacks
Playing leapfrog
Playing marbles
Playing pick-up-sticks
Stepping on a crack meant breaking your mother's back
Toting a buddy on the back or on the handlebars of your bike
Twirling around and around until you got dizzy enough to fall down
Twirling hula hoops

SOME THINGS WE'LL NEVER FORGET:

A rich kid who got more than two bits for allowance

A nickel coke was a beverage in a bottle

Being chosen for the all-star team and then getting sick enough to have to stay home

Buster Brown or patent leather Mary Jane shoes

Standing on the corner clutching your coins waiting for the musical sound of the ice cream truck

Canvas Converse All Stars were the only tennis shoes for any kind of sports

Chasing after the ice truck and getting a chunk of ice

Coaches were always heroes

Collecting ball cards

Favorite teachers

Hoping you weren't the last one picked on choose up

Icy cold summer Kool-Aid

It wasn't cool to wear advertising on your shirt or cap

Lunch boxes sporting your favorites decals

Lying in the snow, moving your arms and legs back and forth to make snow angels

Moms were all at home after school and kids asked permission to visit other friends' homes

Mosquito and chigger bites from outside games

Neighbors watched without a Neighborhood Watch program

New clothes for the first day of school

PTA, Parent Teacher Association, was a family meeting place

Rainy day school games like clap-in, clap-out or heads up, 7-up,or pass it on

Reading with a flashlight under the cover after lights out

Saturday afternoon matinees and saving a seat for your best friend or a girlfriend/boyfriend

Saturday morning cartoons

Secrets you'd *never* tell—cross your heart and hope to die, stick a
  needle in your eye

Shooting at school was with a basketball or in a game of marbles
  or having your picture taken

Sing-a-longs in a car or bus load of friends on the way to a ballgame

Slumber parties

Snagging a long, fly ball in right field and then dropping it

Spam was meat in a can

Spider Man, Superman, Batman and Robin, and Wonder Woman
  were all comic book characters, along with Sluggo and Nancy,
  Archie, Betty, and Veronica

The only bats were wooden bats

Eating a Hershey's bar a square at a time

You didn't get in trouble at school because you knew you'd get in
  worse trouble at home

Watching the basketball roll round and round the rim and
  bounce out just as the buzzer sounds, and your team loses by
  two points

Yes, those were the days we thought would never end.

Somewhere along the way, the kid enjoying the activity became
the mom/dad or the grandma/grandpa, and the cycle of parenthood
continued its never-ending circle as childhood "whens" merged with
the reality of an adult world.

Wasn't it a great trip!

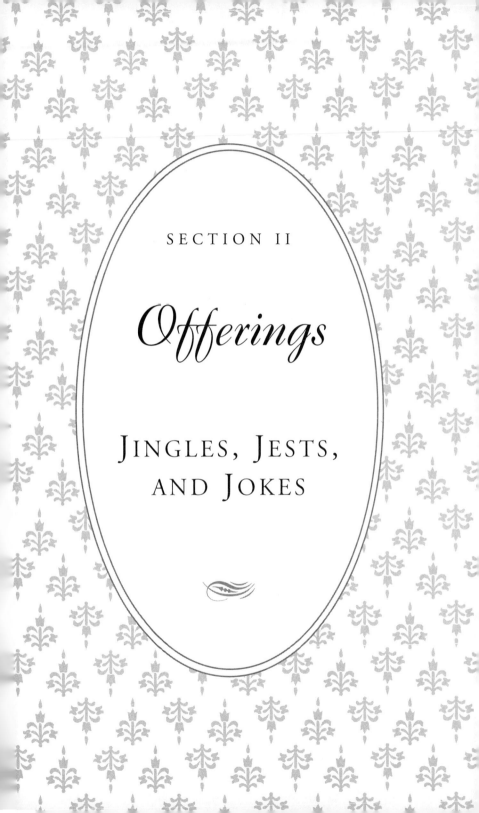

SECTION II

Offerings

JINGLES, JESTS, AND JOKES

ONE

*E*veryone you see is not one,
But everyone you see has got one.
Some have more than one.
Some never know one.
You can't enter life without one,
But you can die without one.
Some step into one.
Some adapt to one.
Some double as one.
Some are a single one.
One can be astounding
And amazing to have around.
Did you know WOW is one
Spelled upside down? ~

CASTLES

My castle stands serenely
On a high and distant hill.
Strong walls command attention
Like soldiers, straight and still.

Stately towers stretch proudly
As giants to touch the sky.
From their tiny windows
I can watch the world go by.

Far below, the river winds
Around a distant bend.
It never stops, but rushes on
Searching for its end.

I built my castle high
With jagged cliffs below.
No one dares to go there
Unless I wish it so.

You see, my castle is a game
I call it make-believe.
Would you like to play with me
My game of make-believe?

CASTLES (CONTINUED)

Just close your eyes
Wish a castle all your own.
Will you build it piece by piece
Or wish it all full-blown?

Perhaps you'd like a moat
With your castle in the center.
A drawbridge to let up or down
So no one else can enter.

Knights in armor, beautiful ladies
Design them in the air.
When you tire of dreaming
You can leave them there.

When my mother calls me
Castles disappear from sight.
I can wish them back again
Whene'er the time is right.

Castles are for visiting
On a cold, lonesome day.
I'd never want to live there
I just go there to play. ∼

GROWING UP

When black was black and white was white
And gray was grown-up ways,
Mom taught the simple, easy things,
Preparing for future days.

Complete trust, undying love,
And faith to always win,
Family, friends, and growing up
Were her whole life, back then.

When my world tinged to adult gray,
I returned to black and white,
Reviewing the simple, easy things,
Teaching my kids wrong from right.

Everlasting love, firm beliefs,
Relying on one another
United my family growing up
During my days as a mother.

When our kids grew up and more kids came
And colored our world with love,
We passed on the simple, easy things,
Giving thanks to the Lord above.

Honest words, continuing faith,
Growing up became a revelation
Passed on from mother to mother
To another generation. ⌒

OLD SAYINGS

*M*y mom used to repeat this old saying. "Mother, Mother, may I go swim?"

"Yes, my darling daughter. Hang your clothes on a hickory limb but don't go near the water."

What does that mean? I wondered.

If I asked Mom, she'd shrug and say, "It's just an old saying."

Of course, when she said it to me, I knew it meant I couldn't go swimming. But why would anyone be foolish enough to strip off and hang his or her clothes on a hickory limb (if they could find one near the creek) and not go in swimming?

Beats me. But, there were a lot of Mom's old sayings I couldn't figure out. How about you?

For instance:

BEAUTY IS ONLY SKIN-DEEP.

Well, I'd settle for that. I always wanted to be beautiful like Liz Taylor. I'd take her, skin and all. I told Mom so.

Years later, after Liz had been through several husbands, had health problems, and was near death, Mom reminded me that beauty had been only skin-deep for Ms. Taylor.

"What did beauty gain her?" Mom asked.

Liz, you may have had your problems, but you sure had a lot of fun having them. And you're still beautiful and probably a lot thicker-skinned, I thought.

BEAUTY IS IN THE EYE OF THE BEHOLDER.

I finally figured this one out (although I spent years wondering what some people could possibly see in other people) after I was grown, married, and became a mother. I had a son who loved dogs, and it all became clear to me.

Reggie never saw a dog he didn't think was beautiful, well, maybe not beautiful, but he just loved dogs. Reggie would pick up a stray dog, bring it home, and, let's be honest, it would be awful. It was usually a mutt, straggly and downright ugly. But, he would hose it off, feed it, pet it, name it, and it was his faithful servant. I would get the family posed for a picture, and there was the mutt huddling at Reggie's feet, drooling up at him admiringly.

Reggie is grown now. He is married and has children of his own who love animals. As a grandmother, when I sort through my long ago pictures of Reggie and his dogs, I look a little closer. I can see the love flowing between a boy and his dog, and it is beautiful. I can finally understand: beauty is in the eye of the beholder.

A BURNED CHILD FEARS THE FIRE.

I learned the meaning of this one by picking up a skillet with a hot handle. I got a second dose of a burned child when I stepped on a discarded fireworks sparkler. Mom had warned me not to go barefooted. I didn't listen, so I learned fear again.

LITTLE PITCHERS HAVE BIG EARS.

The joke is I could never find a pitcher with any ears at all: lots of handles, but no ears. I even thought they were saying little *pictures* have big ears, and certainly some of the ones I saw did have big ears.

Again, when I became a mother, I learned the true meaning of this phrase. Were you ever busy getting ready to go somewhere, see a salesman coming up the walk, and mutter, "I don't have time for this. I'll just not answer the door."

I did, forgetting there was a little pitcher standing nearby in the form of my child. I waited as the salesman knocked. I didn't answer the door. Just as I thought I was home free, my little pitcher ran to the door, opened it, and said, "My mother is not home, and if she was, she's trying to get ready to go somewhere and is not going to answer the door."

Well, kids, I guess you little pitchers come by it naturally. How do you think this big pitcher heard all these old sayings?

I'm sure Mom was once a little pitcher too. It was her big ears a-listening that brought these old sayings to me. ⌢

LABOR OF LOVE

*N*ine long months
Of body changing confusion,
Hours in the labor room
Stretching and bruising.

Losing a perfect body
Amidst screams and tears,
Altering your life
Forever, it appears.

Birthing love's child
Expanding two to three,
Fulfills passion's dream
Creates a family.

Nestled at your breast
Bonding with one another,
Reflected in your baby's eyes
You see a loving mother.

MOTHER LOVE

*O*nce upon a time, a long, long time ago,
  The Master in the Heavens looked on the earth below.
Satisfied with His handiwork, He finished with His plan,
Created in His own image a creature He called Man.

Then, He created Woman, a counterpart of Man,
To live and rule this earth, helpmates, hand in hand.
Each He gave a talent, to each a special place,
Man and Woman, husband and wife, to birth the human race.

Man, as the provider, He gave the urge to roam,
Woman, as the comforter, to bless and keep the home.
A chain of love, so strong, each link needs the other,
Love completes the cycle reproduced by the mother.

Down through the centuries human stories unfold,
Tales of love, hate, revenge, these have all been told.
Values have been twisted that He sent us from above,
If one remains untarnished, 'tis the one called mother love.

I believe God smiles on mothers as they go about their tasks,
When they need His help, they have only but to ask.
Bless you, all dear mothers, when your journey you have run,
As you sit at the Master's feet, you will surely hear, "Well done!"

GRANDMA'S SMILE

A mountain of snow covered her head,
Stars shone from her eyes.
Skin so soft, could it have been
Rose petals in disguise?

Crow's-feet imprinted there, 'tis true
They were left from smiles.
Her ears were caverns to wisdom
Listening to all life's trials.

Her voice, her warmth, her lilting laugh,
With nature all compare.
Hands so versatile, remembered best,
Folded at last as in prayer.

When I retell her tales of old
Or smell a fresh baked pie,
The ache of loss returns within,
I steal a secret cry.

But, as the sunshine warms the earth,
A special ray seeks to atone.
That's Grandma's smile, that seems to say,
"I'm at rest in my heavenly home." ～

DECISIONS

What to get for Mother's Day?
I'd better look around.
I break my piggy bank
Empty it out,
And
Head for uptown.

Which store should I visit?
I'd better think real hard.
I reach into my pocket
Jingle my change
And
Stop to look at a card.

What can I get from a counter
That is labeled notions?
I smell several perfumes
Sample some powder
And
Rub my hands with lotions.

Of course, I could get candy,
I move to look at that.
Mom is on a diet
But if I eat the candy
Then
She won't get fat.

DECISIONS (CONTINUED)

I visit the soda fountain
And eat not one cone, but three,
'Cause I remember all
Mom said she wanted
Was
A hug, a kiss, and me! ～

THE MOTHER TREE

When I was just a little girl
Mamie drew a picture for me
Of a trunk with limbs on it
She called our Family Tree.

She penciled roots at the base
Firmly grounding her foundation,
Drew lower limbs of ancestors
Whose names were our relation.

Offshoots bonded her and Pa
With names straggling out,
Revealing how motherhood
Caused another limb to sprout.

She pointed out Daddy's limb
Joining up with yet another,
That branch added my name
As his wife became my mother.

When I grew up I wanted
To become a Mother Tree!
I'd produce boys and girls
And make family history.

Best laid plans go astray,
Mother Nature needed glasses.
She sent us four study lads
But forgot to send us lassies.

My Mother Tree was full of boys
Who married daughters-in-law
To add names to our branches
Beneath Papa and Grandma.

Now, I'm the one with pen in hand
Adding names to the family tree
As each lady of this generation
Becomes a Mother Tree, like me.

BEAUTIFUL MEMORIES

*A*s a child looking up at my mom, I perceived her as tall. Actually she was a petite 5 feet 2 inches.

Dad used to croon songs to Mom. He'd croon she was his gal, or his woman, or his lady. When he crooned, she had blue eyes.

Wait! Hold on! That wasn't right! "Dad, Mom's eyes aren't blue. They're green," my brother and I would correct Dad.

He'd just grin and sing the song again.

It made me look more closely at the woman I called Mom. *Gosh! She was a beautiful woman!* Slender and olive-skinned, she wore her naturally curly, raven hair atop her head in a loose knot. As she worked, little strings of hair would slip loose and frame her face. She'd try to push them back, but they stubbornly remained, accenting the high cheekbones that hinted Indian heritage.

It always fascinated me to watch Mom redo her hair. Standing, she'd unpin the bun atop her head, letting the length of hair fall to her shoulders and beyond. Gently, she'd brush the dark locks until each tangle was gone. Bending forward, she'd flip her hair over her head and the dark veil would descend. Quickly, she would smooth the sheaf and gather it expertly, twisting the long strain into a coil as she straightened up. Glancing in the mirror, she'd secure the bun with hairpins and try to smooth back the wispy curls that had escaped.

Sometimes, she'd study her facial features in the mirror, pinch her cheeks for color, and maybe rub a little lipstick faintly on her lips, pressing them together to even it out.

Hers was a natural beauty. Her body retained its slender figure because she was instant motion as she moved about keeping her world in shape as she'd been taught to do as a child.

I learned later in life Mom was not of Indian descent—only a native of the red clay of Oklahoma. Her beauty was handed down from her mother. Picking cotton as a child browned her naturally dark skin. Her steel will came from a wiry little gentleman whom we called Pa. Although she and her sisters and brother worked hard helping scrape a living from the Oklahoma soil, it didn't keep the girls from growing into ladies. Her brother grew into a giant of a man.

Mom spoke often of her growing up days, hard work, and lean times, but always there was a light shining in her eyes. Love, family relationships, laughter, and music gave her childhood a cushion. Mom said they didn't have much, but neither did anyone else, so no one noticed.

The songs, stories, and teachings my brother and I learned as children have had an impact on our lives. We pass them on from generation to generation as we call up the image of our mom, the most beautiful person in the world to us. ⌒

HOME

Sweaters flung at the chair
Shoes scattered about the floor,
Banana peels and cookie crumbs
Mark an exit to the door.

Friendly television blares aloud
No audience to hear,
Puppy dog awaits patiently
His master's loving care.

Football kicked in the corner
Replaced by the basketball,
Schoolbooks lie forgotten
On the table in the hall.

A scout book, baseball cards
A poor, wingless fly,
A half-finished model plane
The glue not yet dry.

Laughter amidst pillow fights
Pop shook up to foam,
Disorder, love, and children
Help to make our house a home. ⌒

HAND SPAN

Tiny fingers flailing air
Grasps love's finger tight,
Innocence of babyhood
Fills proud hearts with delight.

Chubby fists a-growing
Question each reply,
Searching, probing, wondering,
What? Where? Why?

Fingernails of boyhood,
Short days leave no time
To fulfill the shocked request
Of removing nature's grime.

Young man's hands a-learning
Wrestles open life's old door,
Steps across his threshold,
A man's world to explore.

A grown man's clasp eludes my own,
Yet, to another clings,
Baby fingers need no more,
Cut loose the apron strings

Tiny fists a-flailing air
The world returns to start,
Ten more little fingers
To wind around love's heart. ⁓

No Instructions Included

Mom's frantic
Doctor comes
Dad's heart jumps!
Nature laughs
As family learns
Junior's got the mumps!

MY LITTLE MEN

What are you, my little men?
Boys, laughing at play?
Or gentlemen dressed for church,
Whispering while you pray?

One minute you're little children,
Your wrongdoings I must scold.
Then next you're helpers, doing tasks
That you've not yet been told.

My little men, you've learned a lot
As you've grown strong and able.
The evidence you can write
Can be found on my best table.

I clean the house for company,
My boys are scrubbed till pink.
Oh! Wet towels on the floor,
Pet turtles in the sink.

When my boys come home no more,
The rooms will be neat, but bare.
It won't be the tables of which I'm proud,
But the names imprinted there.

IMAGES

You met Dad and married before twenty-one,
You built a home and had a son.
Then you learned you'd have another,
The next year I joined my big brother.

Two little kids, a husband, a home,
You'd wash, clean, dress, and comb.
I watched, I copied the things you'd do,
One day I'd be a mom, just like you.

I marveled at the bargains you'd find,
Wherever you went, I was close behind.
You didn't lie, you didn't cheat,
Never said a word I wouldn't repeat.

The songs you sang and books you read
Were lanterns on my path ahead.
You're the greatest mom, one of a kind,
You are my idol. Do you mind?

The stars are brighter in your sky,
If I ever became a mother, I'd know why.
Before I was twenty, I married too,
A home, a family, just like you.

You shared my dreams, recycled my joy,
Became a grandma for my baby boy.
You're happy for me. I'm happy too,
'Cause I'm a mother just like you.

A Mother's Prayer

A mother prayed this prayer at the close of Bible school:
"Thank you, Lord, for using me to be a teaching tool.
Thank you for enduring strength. I've needed it each day.
When faith seemed to falter, I had only but to pray.
We've loved these children, Lord, enjoyed each girl and boy.
Forgive us where we failed. Bless us for each joy.
Just one question, Lord, and it's with love I dare
To wonder at my teaching. Do they really care?
Did they listen, Lord, to lessons that I taught?
Will their lives be touched by scriptures I have brought?
Forgive me, Lord, for doubting, my words sound so unfair,
But, let me see just one thing, Lord, to show they really care."

This mother's prayer is echoed in pure hearts everywhere.
Do the children listen? Do they really care?
As the program ended, an older woman came,
Touched her on the arm, called her by her name.
"I came to talk to you because I felt 'God-led.'"
She put the doubts to rest as these words she said,
"God still answers prayers as the years unfurl,
I prayed a prayer like yours, when you were just a girl." ~

Remember

How far back can you remember?
How many distant days recall
When you were but a child
And your world was mighty small?

Remember eyes
Filled with laughter
Inflated with pride
Strained with worry and
Pain they couldn't hide?

Remember hands
Gentle, always there
Soothing away pain
And folded in prayer
Waiting, welcoming?

Remember love
So freely given
To sister and brother
Weaving a family closer
That memory is mother.

BLOODSUCKING LEECH

When we visited Mom's parents in her home state, we stayed with our grandparents, but we visited all the aunts, uncles, and cousins. Three of Mom's siblings still lived at home. Her other sisters were married and lived nearby, providing us with plenty of cousins to visit.

Rex and I were only a few years younger than one of Mom's sisters. It was hard to believe our grandmother was Aunt Joyce's mom. Joyce was our leader: whatever sermon she was preaching that day, we were her devoted disciples.

On sunny days, we'd start out early and walk to the home of one of Mom's other sisters. It was quite a distance. At the bottom of the hill going up to her place was a branch that ran across the road. We'd stop and soak our feet, then continue on our journey.

While the grown-ups visited, we kids would play ballgames outside. One day as I sat waiting my turn to bat, I reached down to scratch my toe and felt a foreign object attached to the soft skin between my big toe and the adjoining one.

I screamed.

The front door slammed as the mom brigade poured out of the house. The game stopped. I sat on the ground, screaming at a big, black, ugly, oversized tick that was glued to my foot.

Mom took one look at the object and said two words, "Bloodsucking leech."

I was the instant center of attraction. Rex, Joyce, and the cousins edged in to get a good look as the aunts decided whether to remove it or not.

I was yelling, "Get it off!"

As Mom and Joyce pondered the situation, the leech grew fatter and fatter as it continued to satisfy its vampire instinct.

I looked to Joyce, who was my mentor, and repeated. "Get it off!"

Joyce reached between my toes and pulled. It was stuck tight! She pulled again. It budged and popped off. I yelled and screamed. Someone stepped on the leech. My blood, its blood splattered on the ground.

"Boy. He was stuck tight." I breathed a sigh of relief as I examined the red place.

"It's not a he, it's not a she," Mom said.

I loved riddles and that sounded like one. "What does that mean?"

We gathered around as Mom tried to figure a way to explain without using the "sex" word. Finally she simplified it. "God made the leech's body where it could be both the mother and father. Those bloodsuckers lay their eggs in cocoons."

Rex got a stick and poked at the flattened leech. "Wonder how it tells if it's coming or going? Both ends look the same."

"The head end has a disk for the leech to suck blood. The hind end is a disk that's larger so the leech can hold onto objects. That's why it was hard to get off," Mom said.

"Hey, Jane. Let's see where the leech bit you," Joyce said. Everyone gathered around to examine the wound.

"If its head is a disk, how does it bite?" I asked, looking at the wound between my toes.

Mom's sister, who was a teacher, said, "It has a mouth in the middle of the front sucking disc with three small, sharp teeth so it can saw a wound to suck through."

"Yuk!" my cousins screamed and began to search their own feet to be sure they didn't have leeches sawing on them.

The mothers drifted back in the house and the kids resumed their game.

Rex yelled, "Come on and play."

"I can't . . . I'm sick," I moaned.

Joyce came over and looked down at me. "Jane, did you know doctors once used leeches to bleed people to heal them?"

"No." I didn't doubt Joyce. I looked around at my cousins and brother. No one ever doubted Joyce.

With a theatrical gesture, Joyce pronounced, "Consider yourself healed, Jane. Rise, walk, and play."

Once more I surveyed the group. They all nodded solemnly.

I rose, walked, and played. I asked Joyce where I got the leech. She told me I probably got it as we came through the branch.

Later, as we approached the branch on our way home, I ran right through that water. On the other side, I stopped to examine my feet and legs to be sure I didn't have anything attached.

Joyce yelled, "Come on, Jane. What are you doing?"

"Coming! I wanted to be sure I didn't have a leech. One healing a day is enough for me."

Mom hollered, "Hurry up, you girls. Let's get to the house. I want to put some medicine on Jane's foot."

I looked at Joyce. "It's okay, Mom. It's healed."

Mom acted as though she hadn't heard. "I know I brought some iodine in the medicine bag."

Joyce and I both yelled, "Iodine!"

It was Mom's answer for everything.

Grandma said, "Honey, you don't want to put iodine on a leech bite. I've got some salve that'll work just fine."

Mom nodded.

Joyce whispered, "Salve won't burn like iodine."

I breathed a sigh of relief. I was glad Grandma's medicine and advice ranked higher than Mom's (at least while we were at Grandma's home). ⁓

FAMILY ALBUM OF MEMORIES

Ah! The family album.
Ever wonder what makes it so priceless—
Those watermark scenes from the past?
Forever, we're leafing through memories
With kinfolk as stars in the cast.

A jest is a charade of comedy,
Jokes are the stars of the show.
Humor is better than medicine,
If you'll just let yourself go.

Mom's family boasts great joke tellers,
They've mastered the art to a craft.
So, sit back, relax, and enjoy,
You haven't lived till you've laughed.

THE JOKE'S ON . . . WHO?

*M*y mom's family always loved a good joke.
If Mom ever heard a story she really liked, she'd relish telling it at family gatherings. Sometimes she'd insert one or more of the family's names in the joke and make them a part of it. Then she'd say, "The joke's on you!" As the years passed, it was hard to remember if the story was true or a joke. But if it got a good laugh, that was the ultimate goal.

Mom would begin, "My sister, Joyce, and her husband, Ben, used to deliver telephone books in Texas. They were traveling in their car with their trailer hooked on behind. They'd been on the road all morning. Ben was tired and told Joyce he wanted her to drive.

"'Do you think you can handle it?' Ben asked.

"'No problem,' Joyce assured him.

"Just to be sure, Ben charted their route on the map. Then, he retired to the trailer and Joyce took over the navigating.

"Ben removed all of his clothing except his shorts and stretched out on the bed. Soon, he was snoring.

"Everything went well until Joyce got to the outskirts of Fort Worth. Trying to drive and check the map at the same time, she missed her turnoff. She tried to work her way back to the right exit and found herself in downtown Fort Worth."

About this time Mom was working up a head of steam. She'd glance at Joyce and Ben and giggle. Then she'd continue.

"Joyce knew she'd never hear the last of it if Ben woke up. So she decided to do what any sensible woman—but never a man—would do: she looked for the right person to give her directions."

Mom would nod at the rest of the family knowingly.

"Joyce switched to the outside lane and drove as slowly as possible until she saw a tall, good-looking cowboy saunting along the street. Just then the light turned red.

"'Sir, could you help me?' Joyce called."

Mom always emphasized her characters' feelings in a joke.

"The cowboy showed his pearly whites and strutted over to the driver's side where Joyce sat waiting."

At this point Mom paused dramatically.

"Meanwhile, back in the trailer, Ben woke up. He wondered why the trailer was stopped. He walked to the window and pulled back the curtain. There was traffic everywhere. A lady in a car beside the trailer smiled and her little boy pointed at Ben and laughed.

"Ben looked down and realized all he had on were his undershorts. He started to drop the curtain, but his attention was drawn to a tall, sneaky-looking cowboy, standing near the front of their car, grinning like an ape."

Mom made sure her audience noticed Ben's conception of the cowboy was a little different from the way Joyce saw him.

"'What the heck is Joyce doing in the middle of town in all this traffic chatting with a gigolo?' Ben growled.

"Quickly, he went to the back of the trailer and opened the door to investigate. As he started to climb out, horns started to honk. He looked down and saw he'd forgotten to put on his clothes.

"In the driver's seat, Joyce listened as the cowboy graciously pointed out the route to get her back on the right road.

"'Thanks!' she said, just as horns started honking and she realized the light had turned green.

"She waved, accelerated, and pulled ahead thinking, *Now, I'll get back on the road and Ben will never know I got lost.*

"In the trailer, Ben started to turn back and grab his pants just as Joyce pushed on the gas. The car and trailer jerked forward; Ben was thrown backward. The trailer door flew open and he lost his balance, seesawing on the step and immediately finding himself standing in the middle of honking traffic.

"'Damn!' he yelled as he turned to crawl back into the trailer. But the trailer was just turning the corner down the street.

"Angry voices yelled threats about indecent exposure and threatened to call the cops.

"Mortified, Ben realized he was standing in the middle of 'God knows what town' in a traffic jam with nothing on but his underwear."

At this point Mom would look at her sister with the reminder, "Remember Mom always told us to wear clean underwear 'cause we might be in a car wreck? I hope you passed this bit of information along to your husband." Mom would wait until the laughter ceased. Then she continued.

"Ben sprinted for the sidewalk, thinking maybe he could run to the corner and catch Joyce before she got away. Disregarding the amused looks of pedestrians, he reached the corner, but the trailer had vanished.

"'Can I help you, sir?' a female voice yelled.

"Ben turned and saw an attractive policewoman near the curb, straddling a motorcycle.

"'My wife and I were delivering phone books and . . .' Ben began.

"The policewoman shook her head in disbelief.

"Ben finished desperately, 'If you could just follow this route, we could catch her. I can prove what I'm saying.'

"'Hop on,' the policewoman ordered and handed him a helmet.

"Ben pulled on the helmet. Gingerly, he crawled on behind her.

"'You better hold on,' she said.

"He encircled her shapely waist and leaned close, glad to hide as much as possible.

"The policewoman swerved in and out of traffic. She made good time in spite of the commotion they caused. Soon, she spotted a car ahead with a trailer behind it. 'Is that your vehicle?'

"Ben peered around her helmet. 'Yeah. That's it. See the back door is still flapping. What's my wife doing in the middle of Fort Worth, anyway? How dumb can you get?'

"The policewoman turned and looked at him. 'You tell me.'

"Ben didn't say another word.

"Meanwhile, Joyce had almost reached the road that would put her back on their route. She breathed easy. *Now, Ben will never know I messed up. If he ever finds out, I'll never hear the last of it. I wish, just once, Ben would do something I could tease him about.*

"Joyce heard a siren behind her. 'Oh, no! What have I done now?' Horrified, she realized the siren would wake Ben in the trailer. She eased to the side of the road, praying for a way to get out of this predicament.

"There's an old saying, 'Be careful what you pray for, you might get it.' In this case it was true.

"Joyce was already planning what she'd tell Ben as she stopped, opened the door, and started to walk around to the back of the trailer. Suddenly, a motorcycle pulled around the trailer. On it sat an *overly plump policewoman* with someone hugging her waist. The motorcycle stopped. A tall man carefully scooted off the back of the cycle. He walked toward Joyce, naked as the day he was born except for a motorcycle helmet and a pair of spotlessly clean undershorts which looked vaguely familiar."

Mom smiled at the laundry praise she'd inserted for her sister.

"Slowly, he pulled the helmet off and handed it to the policewoman.

"'Ben, is that you?' Joyce could hardly believe her eyes: the man was her husband!

"Ben grunted, 'Don't ask.'

"The policewoman winked at Joyce.

"Joyce was always quick on the uptake. She turned to Ben and said, 'I won't ask if you don't ask.'

"Ben nodded and headed for the back of the trailer."

Mom waited until the laughter and teasing stopped. Then, she finished solemnly, "To this day, Joyce and Ben have never spoken of it to each other. I would never have known this story if a little bird hadn't told me. And, I promised I'd never tell."

They say truth is stranger than fiction. I guess a mixture of the two comes out about like Mom's joke. ⌒

PROMISES

You promised me the moon and stars
When you professed your love.
You'd climb the highest mountain,
Shout it from above.

Jewels, there'd be no end to these,
For furs I'd never pine.
The largest of the castles,
These things would all be mine.

Promises are precious things,
But love and youth are bliss.
I didn't need the moon and stars
We settled for a kiss.

Time has passed and love has grown.
Let's see just for fun,
How many of those promises
You have really done.

The kids are stars, you're my moon
In our sky of love.
The mountain is the pile of bills
You keep our heads above.

The jewel's on my left hand,
The most precious one I've seen.
If our home were any bigger,
I'd never keep it clean.

My memory says that leaves the furs,
With one I'd be content.
Our anniversary's coming soon,
But, dear, I'd never hint.

He says, "Happy Anniversary,"
And then hands me a note.
I open it in wonder.
This is what he wrote.

"The fur has not been made
That would match our budget, dear.
How about another kiss?
Better luck next year!" ⁓

TAKE THAT!

*M*om thought it was only fair to share. So here's one more of her "joke-stories" with Aunt Molly and Uncle John inserted in the joke.

As a child visiting Aunt Molly and Uncle John, I was warned to be nice. Uncle John was a preacher's son. He and Aunt Molly are dedicated church members. All that didn't affect their sense of humor one bit. Aunt Molly told some of the best jokes I have ever heard and laughed at some of the ones I told that made Mom's face turn scarlet. But one the funniest joke ever told was on Aunt Molly. Uncle John told it to Mom and she never failed to pass it on.

"Molly wore an apron over her dress when she did housework. John had a bad habit of untying the bow each time he passed. She vowed to get even.

"One day John told her he was having trouble with their car and would be working on it. He carried the board on wheels outside to push under the car.

"Molly smiled to herself. She knew exactly how she'd get even. She waited awhile to give him time to get on the board and under the car, and then she went outside.

"Molly walked over to where the legs were sticking out from underneath the car. She leaned over and pulled down the pants zipper. Then, she zipped it back and unzipped it again.

"She continued this procedure, gleefully crying, 'Take that, take that, take that!' Until, she looked toward the back door and saw John coming out of the house carrying a radio."

At this point Mom would be overcome by laughter. She'd stop and shake her head, trying to regain her voice so she could continue.

"The board started to wheel out from under the car.

"Molly ran for the house yelling, 'John, who's under the car?'

"John was laughing so hard he was barely able to tell her. 'The preacher came by. He said he knew how to fix the car so I went in to bring out a radio to liven things up. But it looks like you've already taken care of that.'

"The preacher got so excited, he hit his head when he wheeled out. He blacked out and, to this day, he doesn't remember Molly's joke that backfired on her.

"But John does and he tells it every time he gets a chance. Molly doesn't care as long as he quits untying her apron and doesn't tell the preacher."

Mom laughed along with the rest of the family. Molly and John just endured and shook their heads, smiling. They knew their turn to get even would come. It generally did! ⌣

Mean Old Mom

You and I both have a mother.
That's
A proven fact.
They're the ones in charge of
Teaching
Us how to act.
I bet my mom was meaner than yours.
She
Threw a fit
Just because I broke her vase
And
Yelled, "Shit!"
I had to listen to storybooks
That
She read to me.
Homework came before movies
Most
Certainly.
When I wanted pizza for breakfast
She
Nixed that too.
Eggs, cereal, milk, and toast
Simply
Had to do.
Tattoos weren't an option
'Cause
She said, "No!"

I couldn't smoke, drink, have sex
    Because
      She said so.
My best friend really wasn't best
    Without
      A doubt.
Mom could have told me that
    But
      She let me find out.
When everyone else got to lay
    Out
      All night,
I had to be in by curfew because
    Mom
      Thought it wasn't right.
Marriage was the right thing
    No
      Live-in stuff.
A home, husband, children,
    I
      Had it rough.
Now, I'm the meanest mom in town
    Yes
      That's right!
Clean up your plate, pick up your toys
    Almost
      Caused a fight.
Love means mothers don't give in
    Although
      Everybody else's do.

It's different seeing through a mother's
        Eyes
        When mother is you.
Tell your mother you understand and love her
        It'll
        Be music to her ears.
'Cause that's what keep her going
        Just
        Knowing someone cares. ⁓

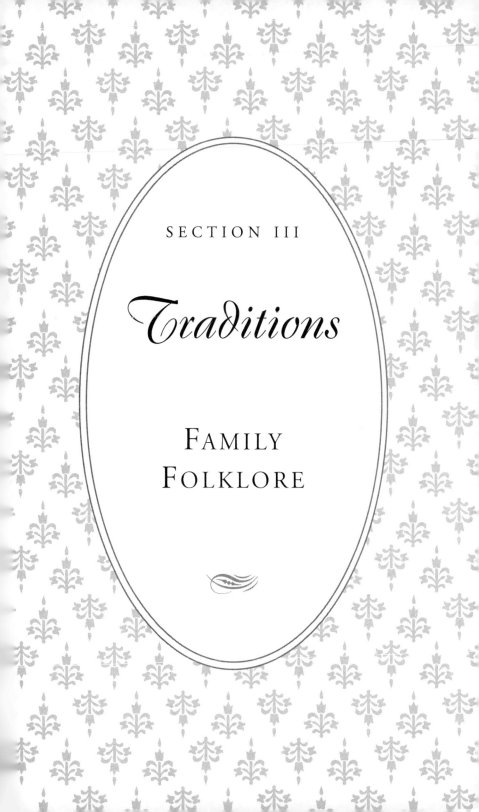

SECTION III

Traditions

FAMILY
FOLKLORE

April Fool

Mom asked, "Did you eat the last cookie, Jane? The one I distinctly told you not to eat?"

"No, Mom, I never touched the cookie. Rex might have. Did you tell him not to eat it too?"

My brother had left the table but was within hearing distance. He immediately proclaimed his innocence. "I didn't eat the cookie!"

Mom leaned down, moistened her finger with saliva, and wiped the corner of my mouth. "Jane, you have a smear that looks like chocolate on your mouth. How do you explain that?"

"It's probably spinach, Mom. You told me to eat all of my spinach. See, Mom, my plate is clean, no spinach."

Rex wandered back to the table and came to my defense, sort of. "Maybe after Jane ate her spinach, she needed something sweet to take away the taste."

I looked at my brother to gauge his words. He screwed up his face and shuddered, expressing my feelings for spinach exactly.

I grinned at him silently, signaling my thanks for his help. "Mom, I needed that cookie to take the taste of the spinach out of my mouth." I breathed easier now that I had told the truth.

I grinned up at Mom, but she wasn't there. She was crossing to the cabinet. She reached up and took down the switch—the dreaded switch that could make you dance! I could feel that cookie churn in my stomach. I looked to Rex for help.

Rex shuddered again and mouthed these words, "Don't lie. You know I didn't eat that cookie."

I should have known. My brother had laid a trap and I had fallen into it. As he started toward the back door, he glanced back and shook his head as if to say, Pay the piper.

I danced the "switch jig." With each jump and hop, I thought, *I'll never tell another lie.* Jump! *I'll never eat the last cookie when Mom tells me not to.* Hop! *I'll never tell Mom I didn't eat the cookie when I did.* Jump! Hop! Jump! *I'll never, never, fall into my brother's trap again.*

But, never is a long time.

"Thou shalt not lie" was a commandment ranking high on Mom's lists of *do nots!* Even little fibs were not tolerated by my mom. So when I found out about April Fools' Day and realized it was acceptable, at certain times, to tell a whooper, I plotted to get even with my brother.

The morning started off fine with Mom catching Dad in an April fool joke.

"No breakfast today. It's too fine a day. I'm going shopping," Mom said as she headed toward the door with her coat on.

Dad, Rex, and I sat at the kitchen table waiting to eat. Our mouths dropped open. *Was the world coming to an end? Our mom was not fixing our breakfast. Instead she was going shopping.*

Mom even went out to the back porch to make her joke seem more real, but she came back in, carrying jelly and jam jars. She twirled around and discarded her coat. Underneath she had on her housedress and apron.

"April fool! You should see your faces." Mom pranced around the kitchen, pulling things out that she'd hidden to make her joke more real.

"Jane, close your mouth and get up and put the plates on the table. April fool!" Mom was giddy with excitement.

Dad slumped in his chair. He was generally the one pulling the pranks. He didn't like being on the other end of a joke.

"April fool! April fool!" Mom sang as she placed everything back on the table.

"So, Mom, it's okay to tell a lie if it's on the first day of April?" I asked as I placed the salt and pepper shakers in front of Dad.

He winked at me and watched as Mom tried to explain the April

Fools' Day custom.

At school, I sailed through the day, telling lie after lie and yelling "April fool!" It was all right because everyone else was doing it too.

At home that evening, I decided to even the score with my brother. "Rex, you know your ball cap, the one Uncle Don gave you? The cap you never take off? The cap you even wear to sleep if Mom doesn't catch you? The one Mom told you to leave home today so she could wash it?"

Rex gave me a get-on-with-it look. "What about my ball cap?"

"Well, Mom got it caught in the wringer on the washer and it doesn't have a bill anymore." I started laughing as I watched him run to the back porch where Mom was taking the wash down from the line.

"Mom, Jane said you ruined my ball cap!" I could hear tears in his voice.

Mom turned and produced a miraculously clean ball cap. You had to look closely to see it was the same one Rex had grudgingly left at home that morning.

Rex pulled the cap over his ear and turned to me. "Liar, liar, pants on fire."

Mom was heading in the direction of the switch cabinet.

"April fool! Rex, Mom, April fool!" I cried.

Mom stopped in her tracks. Rex turned in disbelief.

Yes-s-s-s! I had pulled it off.

When Dad came home, I could hardly wait to tell him my joke. He laughed. All evening we pulled little April fool jokes on each other. What a fun day and Mom had started it all!

The next night as bedtime approached, I roamed the kitchen for a late snack. Seeing the cookie plate, I reached out and devoured the next to the last cookie.

Oops! The cookie I had eaten was the one Mom had told me to save for my sack lunch tomorrow. The last cookie lay lonely on the plate—the one Rex would take to school in his sack lunch. Quickly, I scooped it up and ate it.

I turned to go to bed and saw my brother standing in the door, watching me. Hastily, I tried to wipe away the telltale crumbs.

He glanced at the empty cookie plate. "Did you eat all the cookies? The ones we were supposed to take in our lunch tomorrow?"

"Nope!" I said and grinned. "April fool!"

Rex's eyes narrowed and he smirked. "April fool is done and passed. You're the biggest fool at last!" He turned toward the living room where Mom and Dad were listening to the radio. "Mom-m-m!" ∼

A TIME AND SEASON

*G*randma introduced me to gospel music as she rocked me. I'd nestle against her bosom, breathing in the smell of chocolate chip cookies and lilacs. I was soon sleeping with the angels.

I loved Grandma in a special way. She always shared herself with me. She knew the answers to all my questions. If her answer didn't satisfy me and I continued to ask why, she'd answer from the good book.

"For everything there is a time and season."

I remember sunny summers at my grandparents' farm. It was a busy place, but Grandma always found the time to laugh at my jokes, put a bandage on my hurts, and seal it with a kiss.

There was an endless supply of pets on the farm. My special pet was a puppy named Tag. We were friends. He'd roll over so I could tickle his tummy. Then he'd give me warm, moist kisses with his friendly tongue. I loved him!

When I was six, I cried because I was afraid to go to school. Grandma took me into her living room and showed me the long line of school pictures that decorated her walls. "This row is reserved for you. School is a place for learning. Always do your best and remember, for everything there is a time and season."

I learned to love going to school. I made a lot of new friends. As I grew older, I visited many of their lovely homes. School pictures didn't decorate their walls. The Bible wasn't the main book on their reading table. I found questions without answers. I returned to my source of strength, Grandma.

Grandpa died while I was in high school. The family gathered at the farm to grieve. After the funeral, I stayed with Grandma. She sat on the porch in her rocker and watched while I coaxed Tag from beneath the porch. Tag's eyes looked glazed. He followed my voice and came to me. He wasn't a puppy anymore. I was sad to find his once sturdy body a skeleton of bones. He snapped at me as I reached to stroke his tummy.

Grandma explained to me, "Time passes swiftly. It has been a long time since you were a toddler and Tag was a puppy. Dogs age faster than people. Don't be hurt. Tag has always loved you. Now he is old and wants to rest. One day soon he won't be with us anymore. Do you love him enough to let him go?"

Grandma looked at Grandpa's empty chair on the porch. I knew she was talking about more than Tag.

For everything there is a time and season.

I met the man of my dreams just like Grandma told me I would. I could hardly wait for her to meet him. My world was so full.

We were married and had children. Echoes of my childhood were a reality as I watched the faces of my mother and grandmother as they held my first child.

Time passes swiftly. Grandma got sick. I visited her, taking my first son. His youthful exploration of her home made us both nervous until Grandma said, "Let me take him on my lap and hold him like I used to hold you." He responded to the warmth of her arms and soon fell asleep, just as I had time and time again so many years before.

I looked closer at Grandma and was surprised to find her once sturdy body a skeleton of bones.

As I started to leave, I asked, "Why? Why can't it always be like this, Grandma? I love you so much. I want you to be there for my children like you were for me."

Grandma took my hand and patted it. "Remember Tag?"

And I knew. For everything there is a time and season. ⌒

TRADITION TRIVIA

*I*f you have the mistaken idea your mother invented the phrase, "Goodnight, sleep tight," forget it!

Mattresses as far back as Shakespeare's time were fastened with ropes. If the ropes were tightened, the bed became firmer to sleep on. Thus the phrase, "Goodnight, sleep tight."

"I do" may be the shortest full sentence in the English language but stated at the right time, it dedicates people to the longest sentence in any language.

If the founder of Mother's Day could have looked into the future, she might have opted to change the date of Mother's Day to one of the two days when there is no professional sports game in the NFL, NBA, NHL or MLB.

When is that? It's the day before and the day after the Major Leagues All-Star game.

MOTHER'S DAY

*D*id you ever wonder how Mother's Day became a national holiday?

In ancient Greece, tribute was paid to Rhea, the mother of the gods, with celebrations held in the spring.

During the seventeenth century, England honored mothers on "Mothering Sunday," celebrated on the fourth Sunday of Lent.

In the United States, Julia Ward Howe, a Boston poet, pacifist, suffragist, and author of the lyrics to "The Battle Hymn of the Republic," organized a day encouraging mothers to rally for peace.

A mother, Anna Jarvis, once remarked, "I hope and pray that someone, sometime, will found a memorial mother's day. There are many days for men, but none for mothers."

Two years after Anna Jarvis's death, her daughter and namesake began a campaign to memorialize the life work of her mother. Young Anna Jarvis of Philadelphia is credited with bringing about the official observance of Mother's Day. Jarvis was so moved by the first ceremony held in Grafton, South Virginia, that she began a massive campaign to adopt a formal holiday honoring mothers.

In 1910 West Virginia became the first state to recognize Mother's Day. A year later, nearly every state officially celebrated the day. In 1914 President Woodrow Wilson officially proclaimed Mother's Day as a national holiday to be held on the second Sunday of May.

White carnations became a symbol for mothers. When women sold the flowers to raise money at a 1923 Mother's Day Festival, Jarvis became enraged by the commercialization of the holiday. "This is not what I intended," Jarvis said. "I wanted it to be a day of sentiment, not profit!" Jarvis filed a lawsuit to stop the commercialization. She was arrested for disturbing the peace.

Many celebrations of Mother's Day are held throughout the world. Countries such as Denmark, Finland, Italy, Turkey, Australia, and Belgium celebrate Mother's Day on the same day as the United States. This holiday has become the most popular day of the year to dine out. Telephone lines record their highest traffic as sons and daughters reach out to their mothers on her special day.

It's ironic that Anna Jarvis, who dedicated her life to stopping the commercialization of Mother's Day, may have paid the highest price of all because she never became a mother, herself. But on every Mother's Day, her room in a nursing home, where she died in 1948, was filled with cards from all over the world.

Jarvis told a reporter shortly before her death, "I'm sorry I ever started Mother's Day."

Despite Jarvis's disappointment with the way people chose to celebrate the day she founded for the recognition of mothers, there's a world of children who appreciate a day to express their love for that very special person in their lives, their mother. ⌒

WATER: WHO NEEDS IT?

*M*om said, "You kids need some exercise. Fill these buckets with water and carry them in for me." Mom knew it wasn't a favorite job so she spiced it up. "Pumping water will give you strong muscles."

"Does that mean we won't have to eat spinach?" I asked.

Rex shook his head. He already knew the answer to that question and it wasn't yes.

"Mom, do you think we'll ever have running water in the house?" Rex asked. Several of our neighbors already had inside water.

"Someday, maybe. But for now, we have a pump. Be glad you don't have to draw water out of a well," Mom said.

My brother and I looked at each other. We knew exactly what Mom was talking about.

Mamie, our mom's mother (we also called Dad's mom Mamie), still drew her water from a well outside. The well had a round wall built around it and a roof. A bucket with a long rope attached was lowered into the well until it splashed into the water far below. When the bucket filled with water, it had to be pulled or drawn with a pulley back to the top.

We used to watch Uncle Don draw the water. He made it look like fun. We begged to do it. He finally let us. The first few times we got to draw water from Mamie's well, it was fun. After that, it was hard work. We knew why Uncle Don agreed to let us help. Later we read *Tom Sawyer* and knew Uncle Don's ploy had been used before.

Dad bought Mom a wringer washer, but we still pumped and carried water to fill the washer. When the washer was filled to capacity with water and clothes, it lurched around the porch with a rhythm of its own. The wringer that squeezed water from the clothes was a greedy monster, which would gobble up our fingers if we weren't quick.

Clothes dryers were in the distance future, so Mom hauled baskets of damp laundry to the outside clothesline. She secured the garments with clothespins, allowed them to dry, and carried them back inside to be folded. Nature scented our clothes with a natural fragrance. When the towels, tea towels, undergarments, and unironed clothing were stored, the house smelled like all outdoors.

The ironing was another chore that Mom could not accomplish without water. She used water to make starch for the stiffening of garments. She sprinkled many of the clothes before they were ironed. Those were the days of starched dress shirts and men's pants, which were creased. Mom carefully ironed dresses and hung them in the closet for a single wearing.

The ritual of bathing was observed in most households once a week. Throughout the week Mom stressed sponge bathing, consisting of a damp washcloth applied to nooks and crevices. Saturday night was bath night. The water was warmed in the big reservoir on Mom's cooking range. Our kitchen became our inside bath as a portable tub claimed its rightful place. Fluffy towels, bars of soap, and shampoo were handy.

Because of the hardship of carrying, heating, and emptying the tubs of water, sometimes one tub of water cleaned the whole family. Mom assigned the order of bathing by cleanest first and so on to the one considered the dirtiest. Then, she'd gather the wash things, empty and store the tub, and put her kitchen to rights. Her family was bathtub clean for another week.

The outhouse was located a short distance from the house. In the winter, slop jars were the fashion, but they were the dickens to empty.

Mom wanted us to pump and carry in the water *now.* We knew how long it took to supply the amount of water she needed, and we had been planning to play ball with the gang.

Mom tried another tactic. "Carrying water sure is a body builder. How do you think your uncle Don got those big muscles to pitch baseball?"

Rex perked up at the mention of his idol, Uncle Don.

"Really? Pumping water makes baseball muscles?"

Mom smiled. "Really!"

Thinking I was off the hook because I didn't need muscles like Uncle Don, I started back in the house.

"Jane! You can carry the buckets in while I pump." Rex said.

"I bet Uncle Don carried the water in the house for Mamie. I bet that really gave him big muscles." If it worked for Mom, it should work for me.

"Do you want to play ball with us when the gang comes over?" Rex asked.

"Sure!"

"Then you better think about carrying the buckets." Rex delivered his ultimatum.

"I lined the buckets up in a row. I placed one under the waterspout so the water would flow into it.

Rex started to pump. There was a method to getting that pump to give up water. It took at least three or four up-and-down pumping motions to get a trickle of water started into the bucket. Once the water started running, if you kept pumping, the water would continue running into your bucket.

Mom had warned us to fill the bucket about half full. That way the buckets wouldn't be so heavy, and when we carried them into the house, water wouldn't slosh over the sides onto her linoleum floor.(She was really particular about her floors.)

I started to move the first bucket and replace it with an empty one.

"Wait! Let it get full. It won't take so many buckets. We'll get through faster." Rex kept pumping. "Now! Grab it. Hurry!"

I tugged the heavy bucket aside and pushed the next one under the running water.

"Mom said to only fill them half full." I protested.

"Don't you want to get through faster so we can play ball?"

"Sure!" I huffed and puffed, lugging the bucket with both hands.

Soon we had all the buckets full. Now all we had to do was carry them inside and start filling the places Mom needed water.

I tried to match Rex's rhythm. Lean down and pick up the bucket by the handle. Walk, slosh, walk, slosh until you got to the back door. Set the bucket down. Try to hold the door with one leg while you picked up the bucket and scooted inside. Mom didn't like the screen door open too long, especially in the summer, because flies would get inside. We knew who would spend all day swatting them, so we hurried in and out the door.

We almost had the first bunch of buckets inside and emptied when we heard the gang coming to play ball.

"Hurry, Jane." Rex pumped harder as we again filled the buckets.

His friends lined up to watch. They marveled at Rex's arms pumping up and down. I scurried around, trying to keep the buckets moving.

His friends tired of watching us and scooted off to the side and started playing catch.

Rex pumped faster. I stumbled over buckets trying to keep up.

We had our second bunch of buckets full and were starting to carry them inside. One of the guys missed the baseball and it rolled over to where I was starting to lift a bucket. I picked up the baseball and slung it back angrily.

Whap! The ball slapped against the boy's glove. I looked up to see the boy shaking his glove hand like it was stinging.

I flexed my skinny arm into a muscle pose. "Wow! Mom's right. Carrying water buckets builds muscles for playing baseball. That's how my uncle built his muscles," I said about the time Rex came back to get another bucket.

The boys had stopped to watch again. They moseyed closer. "Rex, how's your muscles?" I asked in a loud voice.

My brother looked at me as if I'd lost my mind. Then he looked up to see his friends watching.

"Carrying water buckets builds muscles, but pumping water gives you muscles like our uncle Don who plays big-time baseball." I started forward with my bucket.

I could hear a grin in my brother's voice. "Yep. There's nothing like pumping water to build baseball muscles."

Soon, we had a brigade pumping and carrying water.

Mom had been checking out our progress.

We sloshed the last bunch of water buckets onto the back porch, stacked the buckets, and grabbed our ball gloves.

"Rex! Jane!" Mom's voice was filled with disapproval.

We turned and walked back to the porch. The gang shuffled along behind us in a swishing rhythm. Slush, swish, slush, swish. We could have filled another bucket with the water we were shedding as we walked. When we reached the outside porch where Mom kept her washtubs, we splashed through puddles of water to stand in front of her.

"You look like a pack of drowned rats," she scolded.

I looked down at my blouse. It was crumbled and wet. My jeans were worse. They were running water. Rex and the guys resembled dogs on a rainy day that were just getting ready to shake.

"How full did you fill the buckets?" she asked.

Rex looked at me. I looked at the guys.

"Jane was supposed to keep the buckets moving under the pump so they wouldn't get so full." Rex squirmed under Mom's gaze. He twisted his shoe in place and water oozed out the sides.

"Mom, Rex's muscles got so strong and he pumped so fast, I couldn't keep the buckets moving fast enough."

The gang nodded in unison.

One even ventured, "I never saw anyone pump as fast as Rex. That pumping sure has made his muscles strong. I'm coming back to help next time you need water." He moved from side to side, making a splashing noise.

Mom stood with her hands on her hips as she shook her head.

Another kid spouted, "Me too. I'm coming over to get me some muscles just like Rex's uncle so I can play big-time baseball."

A slight smile tugged at the corner of Mom's lips. I felt hope and sneaked a peek at Rex. He was nodding at his friend approvingly.

"So, you all want to build some muscles to play baseball, do you?" Mom coached.

"Yes ma'am!" We all agreed, eager to get to our ballgame.

Mom opened the screen door and motioned us inside. "It appears to me you all did a good job of filling up everything with water."

We all beamed.

Her voice dropped, "Especially the back porch floor." She frowned and gestured to the washroom inside. "Look at my clean linoleum—well, it was clean. Now it seems to be covered with water. I wonder how all this water got in here?"

Silence.

"Rex, you go fetch some mops. If you all really want some baseball muscles, mopping is the job for you!" she said.

We mopped in silence except for the sloshing rhythm of our movements. Swish, slosh, squish, squish.

Just as we finished, Mom appeared at the kitchen door with a platter of cookies. "Anyone hungry for cookies and milk?"

We all grinned.

"Well, wash up and come on in the kitchen." She stopped talking and began to laugh along with us, realizing what she'd just said.

"I guess you've had enough washing for one day." She opened the back door and ushered us outside and handed out the cookies.

"Where's the milk, Mom?" Rex asked.

Mom smiled. "I don't think I've got enough milk to go around. But with all the muscles in this group, you should have no trouble pumping up some water."

We all laughed.

I asked, "Anyone want a drink?"

"No, thanks. I've had enough water for one day." Rex said.

The gang agreed.

Water, who needs it? I thought as we all ran for the backyard to play. I knew Mom did, but I hoped it would be awhile before she needed us to pump and carry more. My muscles were big enough. ⌣

HOME FIRES BURNING

*M*om had an icebox, which was rightly named. Blocks of ice were stored in the top section, keeping the contents cool. The iceman delivered ice daily. In the summer, it was a treat to meet the iceman's wagon and beg a chunk of ice to suck on.

When mealtime arrived, we didn't have to wonder if Mom had stopped by the pizza place or picked up fast-food chicken. We knew she had prepared our meals at home. Fast food was far in the future. What Mom might have considered fast food was store-bought bread, which we called light bread, or butter already churned.

On chilly, winter afternoons when we'd return home from school, the aromas from Mom's kitchen were heavenly. We went kitchen begging and ended up with bread and jelly sandwiches or fresh baked cookies.

"Rex, Jane! Put that food up. You'll ruin your supper."

Remembering her childhood, Mom would often relent and allow us to take our sandwiches outside with us while we did our chores, especially if Dad was going to be late for supper.

After we finished our outside work, we'd hurry back to Mom's domain. If we had lessons to do, we'd settle at the dining room table near the potbellied stove, which radiated heat as it coached the teakettle on top to steam.

Mom would urge Rex to stack some wood behind the stove so Dad could fill it to capacity later that evening. Later, Mom would adjust the damper, banking the fire for the night. It was exciting to watch the stove sides heat to a rosy glow, and we marveled at its ability to contain all that fire.

We also had a stove in the living room that had little side rails on it where we could shuck our damp shoes and socks to toast our toes.

Mom also had a special box at the back of the stove where we were supposed to put our footwear to dry.

Our home was small enough that the two stoves and the kitchen cookstove heated the whole house.

The cookstove was the commanding presence in the kitchen. The top area served as a heat surface where Mom kept her skillets and cooking pans boiling and bubbling with nutritious food. An oven for baking filled one side. The other side was a reservoir where water was constantly warm. Across the top were warming ovens, which kept foods ready for Mom to serve. Mom used the space on top of them for her potholders and heat mittens.

When Dad came through the door, stomping his feet and shedding his coat, he'd grab Mom in a big bearhug and swing her around. Then, he'd follow her to the kitchen asking, "What's for supper?"

Rex and I would hurry to the kitchen, hoping when we finished eating there might be time for a family game or two of dominoes, checkers, cards, or maybe a board game like Monopoly.

The tiny kitchen, its windows steamy with contained heat, became our haven. We were Mom's windows to the world.

When Mom asked, "How was your day?" she really wanted to know. Our stories about community affairs, activities, and friendly gossip were her source of keeping informed. She had outside volunteer activities, but her family and home were her mainstays.

We would listen while Dad told his business stories and sometimes a little joke. Then, Rex and I would tell what happened at school. Mom might chime in with her trip to the grocery store or occasionally a trip with family or a friend to the city. Her time away was limited because she had to be home when Rex and I got home from school.

"Good meal, honey" was a high compliment from Dad.

It was a reminder to us also. "Good meal, Mom!"

Mom smiled as she cleared the table. The well-deserved compliments were the bonus or fringe benefits of her job. Her step was a lit-

tle lighter, and her eyes twinkled a little brighter as she finished cleaning and surveyed her kitchen. Satisfied, she pulled the chain on the
overhead light and left her domain spotless, in readiness for the next
morning's meal.

"Hurry, Mom!" we called from the living room.

Wiping her hands on her apron, she called "I'm coming!" as she
hurried to adjust the damper on the stove to keep the home fires burning before she settled in for an evening with her family. ⌢

You Made Your Bed

*A*n excellent housekeeper, Mom was very particular about her beds. She wanted them made up so-so. The sheets had to be tight and tucked in at the foot just right. The bedspread, crowning glory for the bed, had to be tucked beneath the pillows. A pillow was never removed from one of her beds after the bed was made, not even for a nap. She had extra pillows for naps. Once the bed was made, it was sacred space until the spread was turned down for the next night.

Mom spent hours showing me the correct way to make a bed. As an added incentive, she said, "You make your bed every day. Do a good job, and I'll let you make your brother's bed also."

Needless to say, the second suggestion wasn't a bonus as far as I was concerned, but I didn't say so to Mom. At first, I diligently followed her directions. The sheets were taunt, the pillows so-so. I made my bed just good enough to get me by but not good enough to have the honor of making another bed.

Mom seemed satisfied and quit watching so closely. If I'd get up late, I'd rush through making my bed. Sometimes, I'd leave the sheet wrinkled, but I'd try to smooth the spread so it wouldn't show. Since Mom starched and ironed her cotton sheets, those wrinkles became permanent and were not the easiest things to sleep on. So, one day when I heard the old saying, "You made your bed, lie in it," I thought, *I can understand that.*

Wrong! I learned the true meaning of that phrase from Dad. It didn't have a thing to do with the way a bed is made.

When I was in high school, I wanted to be a pitcher on our girls' softball team. I practiced hard, but since our star pitcher, Teresa Peters, was a natural and two years older than I was, I settled for second base and shortstop. When Teresa graduated, Coach Matthews groomed me, along with several other girls, to fill her spot. I learned a lot of responsibility goes with that position. The coach, the team, as well as the fans, depended on me. I loved it!

I also loved to go on dates. I had met a boy from another town who had asked me for a date to go to Springfield. Wow! Mom and Dad had told me I could go.

But! Coach Matthews showed us the schedule for the Conway tournament and pointed out the night we were to play. He told us to stay in the night before the game so we'd be in good shape.

You guessed it! That was the night I had a date, but I figured since we were going to Springfield, no one would ever know. My friend had a date that night also. They stayed in town and were sighted.

The next day Coach called a meeting and read the lineup for that night. I was pitcher, but my friend's name wasn't on the list. When she asked why, he asked her what she had done the night before.

Enough said. Except! She and a lot of other people knew that I had gone to Springfield, and I was going to be pitching. No one said anything. The game meant a lot to our team, and they depended on me.

I'll never know if it was guilt, pressure, or what, but I bombed out. My control was shot. One pitch went clear over the backstop and a run stole home. Coach never said a word, but he benched me.

The way I played ball certainly couldn't have been from staying out late the night before. The date had been a dud. All I could talk about was the ballgame coming up the next evening. We skipped the show and came home early.

I was home free, or was I?

Dad asked me after the game what had happened. I told him the whole thing. Of course, he didn't realize the coach had told us not to go out the night before the game. The damage was done. I had let the team, the coach, my best friend, my family, the whole town down. I asked Dad what to do.

He said, "You made your bed, you lie in it."

I took the easy way out and confessed to the coach. I apologized and promised it would never happen again. And, it didn't. I tried harder and followed every rule as I tried to earn the trust of a coach I idolized. I didn't like to lie in that bed I'd made full of wrinkled half-truths and broken promises.

I played both softball and volleyball for Coach Matthews. He was a fair man. When he realized I was living up to my promises and giving my best, he gave me one of the greatest gifts I could receive—his renewed trust.

Mom taught me the art of making beds physically. I made my bed every morning as Mom taught me and I tried not to shrink. I eventually did such a good job, *I did* get to make my brother's bed, just as Mom had promised.

Today, I make my bed the minute I get up, although I'm not as particular as Mom was about it. We have percale no-iron sheets that wouldn't wrinkle if I pulled a spread over them, but I always straighten them out.

But, more importantly, I've never forgotten the hidden meaning Dad taught me in the phrase, "You made your bed, lie in it."

MONKEY SOCK CHRISTMAS

*T*hinking back to my childhood, I came upon a Christmas that warmed my heart. Let me share it with you and together may we know the true blessing of the season.

The late thirties and early forties were considered recession years with our country just this side of the big depression with war looming in the future.

Grandpa used to say, "Times are hard, but not as hard as they have been."

Grandma taught us, "Christmas is coming, the geese are getting fat. Please put a penny in the old man's hat. If you haven't got a penny, a half a penny will do. If you haven't got a half a penny, God bless you."

As was the custom, our family celebrated Christmas Eve with dinner at Grandma's. Since most of the family lived close, everyone returned home that night to prepare for the arrival of Santa and share the bounty of the morning as separate family groups.

Mom and Dad whispered Christmas secrets in the front seat of the car as it bounced along the rutted farm road to my grandparents' home. My brother and I sat contentedly in the back, surrounded by gaily-wrapped packages as we watched snowflakes drift lazily toward earth.

We topped the hill and could see family cars already parked in front of Grandma's house.

Inside, the smell of pine blended with delicious smells from the kitchen. Tossing aside our coats, we quickly followed the smell of freshly popped corn. Cousins, needle and thread in hand, were stringing popcorn rings for our contribution to the decoration of a huge pine standing in the corner.

Someone stoked logs in the fireplace, and prisms of light danced, highlighting packages piled beneath the tree. Traditional ornaments were being carefully unwrapped. Many were handcrafted: some beautifully; others crudely done by the hand of a child, now grown. Each had a story that was shared before the ornament found its place of honor on the magnificent tree.

Soon, the tree stood in all its glory.

Grandma called, "It's time."

An expectant hush fell over the darkened room, and a triumphant cheer exploded as the tree was lighted. The room became a fairyland of color reflected in the faces of young and old.

Grandma asked Grandpa to say the blessing each year, although she knew it would always be the same: "Nice tree, pass the meat. We can't open the presents until we eat!"

In the dining room, the huge table was laid with a Christmas smorgasbord. Mom agreed with the rest of the family—"Food enough to feed a starving nation!"

I glanced at my cousins who smiled knowingly. This was another way of saying, "Clean your plate; there are starving children in the world."

Food quickly disappeared, although many professed to be too excited to eat. On the table, clean tea towels were tucked around leftovers that would be enjoyed later.

The great moment had arrived. Uncle Don loudly excused himself as he headed for the bathroom. We all begged him to hurry before Santa arrived.

Moments later, there was a pounding on the front door, bells jingled, and "Ho, ho, ho" resounded on the front porch.

Babies cried.

Children's mouths were silenced as their eyes grew large at the sight of the MAN IN RED.

Santa turned to admonish his reindeer, "Ho, Blitzen, keep the team steady, I'll only be a minute." He stomped his feet free of snow, filling the room with Christmas as he handed out gifts, calling us each by name. Then he was gone. The door was shut against the howling wind and drifting snow.

A short time later, Uncle Don stepped over the children on his way back from the bathroom. He slipped down beside his wife and began to unwrap his pile of gifts. Poor Uncle Don. He missed Santa every year. Yet, as he glanced around the room, his eyes were as cheery as Santa himself.

Stories, eggnog, trips to the smorgasbord, and admiring presents came to an end. Mom helped the ladies tidy up. The men went out to start the cars. We anticipated the return home where Santa would visit later that Christmas Eve.

"Might as well bed down for the night. The snow's too deep to get out," Grandpa's voice warned as the men stomped back inside.

Grandma was already pulling down piles of quilts.

That Christmas, my grandparents' house was packed with family, upstairs and down. Cousins snuggled knee-deep in pallets on the floor covered with quilts.

Grandpa lay snoring on the far side of their bed with grandchildren tucked between him and the place left for Grandma.

Finally, Grandma sat before the fireplace, cradling one of the smallest babies.

Silence descended on the snow-covered farmhouse.

Whispers were cut short as Grandma began to recite the Christmas story, "In the days of Herod the King, Lo! The star came and stood before where the young child lay. They called his name, Jesus! . . ." She finished the Bible verses.

A voice somewhere in the house began singing "Silent Night." Upstairs and down, voices blended in unison. One song ended and another began.

Beneath mounds of covers, a tiny voice ventured, "Up on the

housetop the reindeer pause. Out jumps good ole Santa Claus."

Grandpa got up to stoke the logs in the fireplace, and the room grew quiet. Crawling into bed, he said in a stern voice, "That's enough."

Grandma's voice seemed to smile through the darkness. "Almost," she said, and then she began, "'Twas the night before Christmas when all through the house, not a creature was stirring, not even a mouse."

My eyes closed. My mind drifted. The last words I heard were, "The children were tucked all snug in their beds . . ." In my dreams, I searched the night through for an illusive Santa. In my heart, I knew he would never find his way through the snow to our house.

Someone was shaking me. "Open your eyes, look around."

Rubbing my eyes, I sat up.

The room was full of cousins in stages of wakefulness, all staring open-mouthed at stockings hanging around the room. Hordes of new brown and white monkey socks, the kind Grandpa wore for work, were filled to the brim with goodies. Each bore a name and a single hickory stick.

Mixed with fresh baked bread and cookie aroma, the adult smell of coffee drifted from the kitchen. Aunts, uncles, Mom, Dad, and our grandparents joined us as we found the joy of Christmas stuffed inside monkey socks: apples, shined to a gloss; oranges, a rare treat in the winter; pieces of Grandpa's hard rock candy; fresh Christmas cookies; and a special gift inside for each and every one.

Inside my stocking was Grandma's well-worn storybook I had coveted. My brother pulled out a little box of BB's, forerunner of what Santa might bring. There was a finished quilt scrap for my cousin, who was learning the art of quilting; whet rock to sharpen a Santa-promised knife; and on and on.

The simple joys shared and the hours of labor given made the season one to be remembered.

The snow was plowed. We each returned to our own homes to

find Santa had, indeed, found us. Yet, the memory of the night we were snowed in at Grandma's on Christmas Eve was stored in a special place in my mind.

As years pass, I find solace in that memory. I know, now, the hours of tireless work that went into making the waking hours of children wondrous as I find myself listening to a voice echoing my grandma, "'Twas the night before Christmas . . ."

And, I know the responsibility of age, love, caring, and sharing rests on my shoulders. I must stay awake to finish what generations before me started.

"And we heard him exclaim as he drove out of sight, 'A Merry Christmas to all and to all a good night.'"

God bless you all. ∽

MOM'S CHRISTMAS SHOPPING

*T*One day in December I awoke with a feeling of urgency. Suppressing it, I chose to wrap Christmas presents. As I sat amidst the clutter, it came to me: Mom's Christmas shopping wasn't finished. Each year she had called the bank and requested crisp bills to fill her Christmas envelopes. She would not rest until I picked up the money and the envelopes were ready. Mom was gone, but the urgency persisted.

Mom was a strong, determined person. She lived a widow's life for twenty-six years, devoting herself to her children, grandchildren, and great-grandchildren. We were her world.

Not one to be idle, she could put a strong man to shame with her labors of love until illness claimed her. We wondered at her patience of Job as we cursed the wasting of her body, the loss of circulation in her limbs, and the fluid that necessitated her wearing the hated white elastic hose.

She stored her pride and accepted the wheelchair as a mode of transportation for doctor appointments. She steadily grew worse. We found solace in friends, family, and counsel of professional help. Hospice became more than a word. The parent-child role was reversed as she became solely dependent.

Mom died October 31, 1993.

Our family would have to celebrate our first Christmas without the matriarch who had sustained us for so long. No more special envelopes with little verses to personalize them. No more checking time and again to be sure Mom hadn't missed someone's envelope. No more driving by to pick up Mom for the Yuletide celebration. It was so hard to realize she was gone. It was impossible to imagine Christmas without Mom there, handing out her envelopes and reminding the little kids to tuck their envelopes away for safekeeping.

This year there would be no envelopes from Mom.

"And why not?"

Echoes of Mom's voice lifted the weight of grief as I realized exactly what Mom would want me to do.

"All right, Mom. We'll do it your way," I said aloud.

I called for the money, finished the envelopes, and decided if this were to be her last Christmas, we would do it right.

Using Mom's words and phrases, I composed a verse and enclosed it with each envelope. When the family members opened their presents that Christmas, this is what they found:

Merry Christmas 1993

I probably won't be alive to see it
but I'll be there in spirit.
My old, earthly body has passed away,
Keep my memory with you,
forever and a day.
Now, remember God's teachings,
Don't grieve or cry.
I'll see you again in the wink of an eye!
Merry Christmas to all and to all a goodbye.

If ever there were a fork in the road, completing Mom's Christmas shopping was surely mine. It proved to be a bonding process for all of the family as a Christmas memory finally put Mom to rest. ⌒

Home

A House Is Just a House. Mom Made It a Home.

Beneath Your Mother's Heart

The feeble movement of the child
Stirred love within her breast.
With a voice, so gentle, she crooned
Sweet baby, rest.
In thy cocoon, be patient,
Till nature bids thee depart.
The safest place you'll ever be
Is beneath your mother's heart.

THE CAREER OF A MOTHER

From the love of two people, a baby is created. A tiny miracle grows within the mother until the time when it becomes a separate person. A baby's cry announces its arrival into a new world. Mother's first job is finished—the job of natural mother.

I am the child of my mother and father. I personally know no other life. I lay within her womb for the gestation period of nine months, enjoying the security of her person as I rested just beneath her heart. There are other ways to be a mother, but this was hers. She gave life and, with that life, her responsibility never ended.

Even after death, she counsels me. Her voice is mine. I find her in the morning, bright with promise; in the evening, weary from toil. Her memory remains within my heart, where her teachings are as secure as the umbilical cord, which for nine months linked me to the person on whom I could always depend.

She was first, and foremost, my mother, but, as I search through treasures left from her lifetime, I find the person who was the woman. If I had listened and watched closely, I would have seen glimpses of the woman. I saw the mother. She was both.

Mother told stories of walking miles to school and one day rushing home to tell of the huge, winged bird that swooped over them as she saw her first airplane.

She spoke of working in cotton fields with her family, four sisters and one brother, alongside her mother and father, as they tweaked a living from the Oklahoma soil.

She told tales of her father, a small, thin man with the strength of Samson, whose love for sports and the game of chance has perpetuated itself within his heirs. She shared stories of her mother, the giver of life, who was the solid rock on which the family was built.

My mother was a beautiful young lady who must have left a trail of broken hearts in her search for the right person, my father. When the wedding vows were read, and Mother answered, "I do," she was promising more than just to be a wife. She was beginning a new career. Many women from her generation were dedicated homemakers. It was their way of life.

My mother was a perfectionist. She expected the same from her family. Her home was the cleanest; her family, the best dressed. She was an excellent seamstress and gathered material from feed sacks to bargain counters as she stretched the family budget. Her table boasted the best cooking from the harvest she had reaped.

She encouraged my brother and me to become the best. "Anything is possible if you strive hard enough."

Mother was a support system for our father. She never took the lead in the relationship as was the custom of her day, but she helped, coached, pushed, and loved him as they made their way through life.

My father died in the late sixties, leaving Mother a widow for over twenty years. She never considered marrying again. When she said, "Until death do us part," she was talking about her death, not just my father's.

Mother had always talked of traveling, but after my father's death, she remained close to the home they had made as if his presence resided there. She spent her energies on church work, community work, cleaning, and loving her children and grandchildren.

My mother became MY BEST FRIEND.

As she reached the latter part of her seventies, I found myself assuming the role of parent while she became more childlike in many ways. As she had always been so active, she was desolate when illness overtook her.

In the last three years of her life, we traveled to doctors, hospitals, and finally a nursing home, where the strength of her spirit was evident among others whose minds were wandering.

My mother was buried on her eighty-third birthday, November 2, 1993. At her funeral, my brother and I found her teachings to be true: you can do anything if you try hard enough!

Rex and I became a part of her funeral services as I recited, "Mother," a song she taught me as a child. Then we joined hands, walked the few steps to her casket, and each placed a red rose in her folded hands.

M   *is for the MILLION things she gave me.*

O   *means only that she's growing OLD.*

T   *is for the TEARS she shed to save me.*

H   *is for her HEART of purest gold.*

E   *is for her EYES, like love-light shining.*

R   *means RIGHT and right she'll always be.*

Put them all together they spell MOTHER, the word that has always meant the world to [my brother and] me.

(Howard Johnson, "MOTHER," c1915.)

THE CHAIN LETTER

*M*om asked as Dad placed the mail on the kitchen counter, "Did I get a letter?"

"A couple." He crossed to the porch to wash up for supper. Dad liked to eat soon after he got home from work. Rex was already seated at the kitchen table. I carried glasses of iced sun tea to the table. Mom dried her hands on her apron and hurried to shuffle through the mail.

"Nez, let's eat, I'm starving." Dad was eyeing the platter of meatloaf.

Mom examined her letters. She placed one near her writing tablet and envelopes as was her custom when receiving a letter from one of her sisters. She would read it at her leisure. She brought the other letter with her to the table and laid it near her plate.

We began the ritual of passing bowls around the table.

"I wonder who wrote me this letter?" Mom said as she picked up the envelope and examined it. "There's no return address." She checked the postmark. "It's from Texas! Who do I know in that state?"

"Are you going to open that letter or look at it all night?" Dad knew Mom's inclinations. Mail was of great importance to her. "Let's hope it isn't another coupon offer." His grin was a reminder of the big deal Mom had made of the *last* coupon offer.

Mom opened her envelope while we ate. "Listen to this! 'Please send this letter to seven people after adding your name to the bottom of this list. Enclose a handkerchief in each letter. After several weeks you will receive a multitude of letters with handkerchiefs inside. Another lady who did not continue this letter had a misfortune.'" Mom stopped to look around the table at her family as if imagining what bad luck might befall us if she didn't comply with the instructions.

"That's a chain letter. Aren't they against the law?" Dad asked.

"Not unless they ask for money! My letter only asks for handkerchiefs."

"Why in God's name would you want a multitude of handkerchiefs?" Dad asked as his fork traveled from his plate to his mouth.

"What if I broke the chain and had bad luck?"

Dad muffled his answer, "I guess you wouldn't have a handkerchief to cry in."

Rex and I giggled.

Mom turned, knowing Dad had made some remark.

Rex and I stared hard at our plates.

"And what, exactly, did you say, Mr. Know-it-all?"

"I said this supper is good enough to make a grown man cry. Your food is going to get cold. That's the biggest misfortune that could befall a person. Isn't that right, kids?"

Eagerly we nodded.

That night I awoke thirsty. There was a light on in the kitchen, and I figured Mom was still up doing chores. Dad's snores echoed through the house as I tiptoed down the long dark screened-in porch. Rex did a youthful imitation of the echo.

I raised the water dipper to my mouth.

Mom called softly, "Who's there?"

"It's me, Mom. I was thirsty."

"Come here a minute. I need you to do something for me."

Drat! Count on Mom, even at this hour, to have a job for me. Mom sat at the kitchen table with her writing tablet. A box of envelopes lay nearby. She was in the process of attaching a stamp to the last of a stack of letters.

Oh, no, I thought. *She wants me to lick the envelopes.* Yuk! I had just freshened my mouth with cool water. I could taste the gluey paste.

"Please go in by the ironing board and bring me seven handkerchiefs."

I hurried to get the handkerchiefs, relieved to not have to lick the envelopes. I brought them back to the table. I glanced down and saw envelopes addressed to my four aunts, my two grandmas, and Dad's secretary."

"Thanks, Jane. You better get to bed."

She was sending the chain letter off!

Mom looked up from stuffing an envelope with a lacy handkerchief. "Just think of this as a dream. And, it will be one dream you don't mention to Rex and your dad, understand?"

Boy, did I understand. But it would be so hard to not tell about Mom's saving us from a dreadful misfortune.

As I passed my brother's bed, he growled, "What are you doing up? Who were you talking to in the kitchen?"

"I was thirsty. I don't think there's anyone in the kitchen. But, if there was, it would probably be Mom trying to save us all from misfortune."

As I crawled into bed, I heard Rex get up.

"Where are you going?"

"Since I'm awake, I'm going to get a drink. I'll check out the kitchen."

I was drifting off to sleep when I heard Mom's voice, "What are you doing up, Rex?"

Wow! Good fortune was already smiling on me. I would sleep better knowing I wasn't the only one who was supposed to be dreaming. Mom's chain letters were working and she hadn't even mailed them yet!

POWER OF THE PRESS

*E*ven before I was old enough to leave the confines of the large yard surrounding our house, I had neighbors and sidewalk friends. Our neighbors' yards merged with our own. We were lucky to have good neighbors on both sides.

Between our neighbor on the north and our yard was a big walnut tree, which Rex and I considered a boundary line. It lined up with the public sidewalk that ran across the front of our property.

We always said "Hello" to the people passing by.

Everyone stopped to talk. They told us stories about other neighbors, the town, the school—just chitchat.

A new little rent house went up down the street. The pretty redheaded lady who wore the brightest clothes was added to my list of sidewalk friends. She handed out chewing gum just like the kind she chewed constantly. I had never seen a lady wear high heels all the time. I thought she was something!

Later, I heard my mom and her friend from next door talking. I could tell they thought she was something! I heard Dad and the guys talking and was amazed to find they thought she was something too.

At this time, I was old enough to go out into the neighborhood to promote school raffles and sell Christmas cards. Dad thought it was neat that I was enterprising.

Mom was the one who taught me the sales pitch. "Always start by introducing yourself. Tell your prospective customer who your parents are and where you live. Then say, 'I have something I know you will want to purchase.'"

Then I explained the purpose and what the proceeds went for and how I benefited. By the time I finished my pitch, most of our neighbors were reaching in their pockets, knowing that was the only way they were going to get rid of me. Well, think about it—those were the days of door-to-door salesmen, and possibly my merchandise saved our friends from making a trip to the store or talking with another salesman.

Knowing the neighborhood as I did, I passed everyone's tales along to others while visiting with the sidewalk people and our neighbors.

One day a sidewalk man said, "You're a walking newspaper. You ought to start your own publication."

When I asked him what he meant, he told me how reporters asked people questions, wrote stories, and sold their papers.

Well, great, I thought.

I sat in the front yard under the walnut shade tree with my notebook. When my friends came by, I told them what the man had told me. I asked them if they would want to buy my little paper for a nickel. Of course they would. They thought it was a cute idea.

I soon found a nickel wasn't enough for copying all those stories over and over. So I made my paper short and sweet.

Mr. G. lives across the street from the pretty red-haired lady. He says she has a lot of company, especially at night.

Mr. H. is a schoolteacher. His wife sings.

The redheaded lady gave me some chewing gum. Her friends bring her gum and candy. She is something!

Our next-door neighbor is going to be a baseball umpire! He thinks the redheaded lady is something!

Mr. T. gave me some candy. He asked about my friend, the redheaded lady. I don't know what she does for a living. I'll have to ask her. He thinks she's something too.

About that time, Mr. T.'s wife saw one of my little newspapers. She brought it to Mom, who showed it to Dad, who told me I should shut down my press.

I wondered why he'd make me give up a sure thing.

One day I overheard a conversation between him and his friends.

"Yeah. Jane had to quit her little newspaper. The neighborhood was hearing too much about her friend, the redheaded lady. Jane thought that lady was really something!"

I heard them laugh.

Then, Dad said, "Of course, we all know she is something—except Jane's not old enough to know just what."

I bet if I could have kept my newspaper, I would have figured it out, don't you? You know, the power of the press, the neighbors, and all.

Jeez! I bet that's what Mom and Dad thought too! ⌣

RAW HEAD AND BLOODY BONES

J had my share of childhood injuries—skinned knees and elbows. I learned to endure humongous fever blisters, warts, and the dreaded itch that spread through grade school like the black plague. Mom kept our shots up-to-date—whooping cough, diphtheria, and chickenpox. She thought she had foolproofed us, but I think Rex and I had all of the above, plus mumps.

Mom loved to dress Rex and me in brother-sister outfits, which she designed, sewed, and kept immaculate. Periodically, she'd take us to the local photographer and record our image for prosperity. Mom told me it never failed—when she planned to take us for a picture, I'd always have a skinned knee. Since she dressed me in short dresses and skirts, my sore knee ruined the perfection of her picture.

I don't know about you, but when we got hurt, we ran to Mom (at least until we learned better). Mom kept a fully stocked medicine cabinet of tape, neatly cut bandages, salves, and exotic green and brown bottles.

Roller-skating, running, or riding a bike, I could get a bad sidewalk scrape. I'd be having great fun and suddenly, whap! My knee, elbow, some part of my anatomy was bleeding, hurting. I thought I was dying.

"Waa! Mom. I've injured myself."

The importance of the word *injured* brought Mom running with her medicine. Rex was older than I and wiser by experience. If I hurt myself and screamed for Medic Mom, he sat back to watch the fun. I'd limp a deadly limp toward the house, screaming. The whole neighborhood would open doors to see what had happened.

Mom would run out, see the blood, run back, and return with rags, bandages, scissors, and her medicine.

Her little brown bottle would stop me in my tracks. I'd turn to Rex for help. He'd shrug, smile, grit his teeth, and grimace.

Was there no help?

I'd dab at my injury, attempting to remove the traces, straighten up, try to smile and assure Mom I was perfectly all right. "Hey, Mom. I'm fine. I'll run some water over it and it'll be well. Okay?"

"Come around to the hydrant, we'll see," Mom answered.

I'd do my best to walk tall as I went to the hydrant in the backyard.

Rex followed.

Did you ever run water over a fresh scrape? Did you try not to yell when you were just a little kid? You did, if you wanted to avoid the dreaded little brown bottle.

"Stick that knee under the water. Let's see how deep the wound is."

Oh, no. The *wound!* That sounded worse than injury. I braced myself as Mom turned on the hydrant. I leaned my injured knee closer, closer. The spray of water hit. I closed my eyes, bit my tongue, gritted my teeth, and held onto the scream that threatened to bring the neighbors to their doors again.

Then, I opened my eyes. The wound was deep! The blood continued to run, and Mom was unscrewing the lid of the little brown bottle.

Rex leaned in to get a better look. He shook his head and shuddered. I could hear him mutter, "Raw head and bloody bones!"

And, there it was. The naked skull with the raw bones crossed behind it. The label was plainly marked IODINE!

"Mom . . . no . . . no!" I begged.

Mom poured iodine without hesitation. The pale red liquid tipped the top, splashed over, and headed for my wounded knee that lay exposed, bleeding. The two met with an explosion. No eye closing, teeth clenching, or holding on can control raw head and bloody bones.

I flung my head back and emitted a scream that returned the neighbors to their porches where they stood solemnly shaking their heads in unison as they bonded with my pain.

Mom dashed another splash for good measure.

The deed was done. Time for bravery returned. I swiped the tears away and hobbled to the back porch to have a pity party.

Rex returned to the front yard to resume his play.

The neighbors closed their doors on another episode of raw head and bloody bones.

Mom marched inside, cleaned her medical supplies, and settled the little brown bottle back in her medicine cabinet.

Huddled on an old quilt Mom let us use for naps, I studied my injured knee. Old raw head and bloody bones outlined the gash that gaped open. I knew it would heal, but right now it looked awful.

Mom returned to the porch and I could hear her humming her tuneless little song that came with irritation. In her hand she held a calendar. She shook her head as she silently pointed to the next day's date where she had penciled in, "Take the kids to the studio for pictures."

It never failed!

CHERRIES, APPLES, AND HICKORY TEA

*O*ur cherry tree had the biggest, reddest, juiciest cherries in town. Rex and I shook, poked, and wrestled all the cherries from the lower limbs.

As we watched the birds feast on the best of the fruit in the top limbs, Rex said, "I bet I could climb to the top limbs and get those big old cherries."

"Sure you could," I agreed. "I bet I could too."

Rex thought a minute. "I bet you could go higher because you're a skinny girl. Why don't you shimmy up that tree and pick those cherries? I'll run and get a bucket and you can toss them into it."

I started my climb upward while Rex ran for the shed. By the time he got back, I was on the limbs near the top. Grabbing handfuls of cherries, I dropped them into his bucket. As I continued to throw cherries down, the bottom of the bucket stared up at me. I looked at Rex and saw his mouth was stained with berry juice and his jaws were crammed full.

"Hey! You said we were going to wait until I got down and we'd divide the cherries." I climbed a limb higher and froze as I heard it crack.

"Get down before you break that limb," Rex yelled. "You can have the rest of the cherries."

I grabbed for the limb below me and steadied myself. I snatched a handful of cherries and stuffed them in my mouth as I continued to toss handfuls to the bucket. As long as I was up there, I might as well get the cherries instead of letting the birds have them.

"Rex Juan! Myra Jane! What do you think you're doing? Didn't I tell you not to climb that cherry tree?" Mom was standing near the back door, her hands on her hips. That stance usually meant *trouble*.

Rex began his explanation, "Jane wanted some cherries and she thought she might be skinny enough so those little limbs would hold her."

Mom had picked up a switch from beneath the tree and was advancing toward Rex, who was busy trying to keep his distance.

"Mom, we were just trying to get some of those cherries you wanted. Remember the ones you said the birds always got?" I reminded her.

"Myra Jane, what I remember telling you kids was to not climb the cherry tree. Do you remember what I said would happen if I caught you climbing the cherry tree?"

Boy, did I remember! I was trying to get down as fast as I could while watching Rex get what I could imagine was a preview of the coming attractions for me. I was screaming bloody murder before my feet hit the ground.

A few days later after the stinging had gone away from our legs, Rex and I were once more in the backyard. We gave the cherry tree a wide berth.

Rex stopped beneath the apple tree and looked up. The sunlight glinted off two large red apples at the top of the tree.

"Jane, look at that big red apple near the top of the tree. It looks like it's got your name on it."

I peered up, but try as I might, I couldn't see any writing on that apple.

"Hey, that big one by it has got my name on it. I might just go up and get my apple. Would you like to have yours?"

Boy, would I? I could taste that red apple already.

"You're a lot better climber that I am. I bet you could be up there and back before I got halfway up. But, I guess I'll try," he said.

I already had my foot on the first limb. About halfway up, I scraped my leg, causing it to sting like the switching I'd had earlier in the week. Remembering, I started down.

"Hey, you didn't get the apples. Did you forget?"

"What I didn't forget was what Mom said she'd do if she caught me in a tree again," I said.

"Think, Jane, you've got it wrong again, as usual. What exactly did Mom say?"

I rested in the fork of two good-sized limbs and thought about it. "She said if she caught us climbing that cherry tree, we'd get a good dose of hickory tea."

"Hey, you got it right! She said the *cherry* tree. Did she mention the apple tree?"

No, come to think of it, she didn't. I started my climb back up, straining to see my name on the apple.

"Hey, reach out and tip my apple down. I bet I can catch it before it hits the ground."

I swatted his apple, staring to see "Rex" printed on it as it fell. It went by so fast I missed it. Sure enough, Rex reached out and made a beautiful catch.

"Does it have your name on it?" I yelled.

"It sure does!" Rex answered as he ran toward the shed, munching as he went.

I could taste my apple. I reached out and picked it, turning it in my hand to see where my name was.

"Myra Jane!" Mom stood beneath the apple tree, switch in hand.

"Hey, Mom, I was just trying to see my name on this apple."

"Young lady, do you remember what I said about climbing trees?"

"Boy, do I, Mom. You said not to climb the cherry tree. This is an apple tree, Mom." I looked down to see if she understood. I watched her face turn the color of my apple.

"Missy, a smart aleck gets a double dose of hickory tea. Now get down here, fast."

"But, Mom!" I looked around for Rex.

A blur of color caught my eye near the shed. Rex was sitting on the ground—leaning against the shed, munching his apple. If I told on him, I knew he'd get even.

"Myra Jane! Get down here," Mom repeated.

I hit the ground running and headed for the shed. As Mom and I rounded the corner, Rex was just preparing to toss his apple core.

"Rex Juan! Where did you get that apple? Have you been egging your sister on to climb trees again?" Mom took a practice swipe at Rex, causing him to leap full-blown to his feet.

"Mom, I didn't climb a tree. I was on the ground when I got my apple." Rex told his version of the truth.

While Mom served up my brother's hickory tea, I turned my apple over and over, trying to find "Jane" printed on it. All I saw was my reflection in the shiny skin of a red apple. I looked up to see Mom coming my way, and I knew if my name were on anything, it was the switch in Mom's hand. For once I was right. ⌣

HOME PLACE

Home Place Dedication

Home Place was written in memory of the daughters of Lee and Becky Hale: Molly (Hale) Dodson, Hazel (Hale) Deck, Hildreth (Hale) Wells, and Fredia Hale.

Completing the Hale family were the sons: Lyndell Hale and Dean Hale, who was the father of Bill, Shirley (Hale) Weatherly, Louise (Hale) Smith and my husband, Bob.

*T*he sisters returned home yesterday. They hadn't received their mail at this address for over a decade, but at the sight of the old two-story house, their hearts immediately spoke the words *Home Place.*

Over the years, what had once been their entire universe had shrunk to life-size small. The town had grown and engulfed the country pastures. The neglect of the renters was evident. Pursing their lips in distaste, they silently agreed—Papa and Mama would not approve.

Their footsteps followed well-remembered paths of childhood to the barn at the back of the property. Papa's hands had built this barn. He was a carpenter by trade and a farmer by necessity.

Arthritic fingers clenched with remembrance as the sisters gazed around the small building filled with a stranger's debris. Little girls' hands had helped squeeze milk from old Bossy, carry the milk to the back porch, strain it, skim it, and churn it to butter. Much of the family food was a labor of love.

Swallowing hard, they retraced the path to the house. Their eyes searched for landmarks. What had happened to the chicken house?

"Mama, it's Elza's turn to gather the eggs; I did it yesterday," Josie's childish voice echoed from the past. Josie sneaked a peek at her sister,

Elza.

"Yes. I remember." Elza scolded. "You always gathered the eggs *yesterday.*"

The cellar, which doubled as a storm shelter, was the storehouse for family food. Fresh apples, pears, and other fruits from the orchard kept the little room fresh with a tart, pungent smell. Rows of shelves stacked neatly with canned goods had served the family table well.

"Humph. Looks like someone used it for a trash dump!" Josie twitched her nose.

The kitchen beckoned. The aroma of Mama's home-baked bread, fried apple pies, and blackberry cobbler enticed them. Nothing ever smelled as good as Mama's kitchen when they'd race home from school and fling open the door in anticipation of the goodies that awaited them. All of her specialties were cooked with no preservatives added. Just love.

A vision of Mama, wiping her hands on her apron in preparation for a hug, was gone in an instant. Huddled together, they stared in disbelief as sunshine cut through the grimy windowpanes, highlighting worn-out appliances, warped cabinet doors, and empty shelves.

"Old Mother Hubbard went to the cupboard . . . ," Josie recited.

Elza blinked back the tears that rushed to her eyes as she stepped into the dining room. It had been used for Sunday company and everyday fellowship. Here the family had gathered after the chores and supper were finished. Stories of the day were shared, along with a Bible verse or a book before early bedtime. Farm chores demanded attention before the rooster crowed at first light.

The family table and chairs had been removed years ago. Mama's china cabinet and dishes had been stored. The walls were bare of family pictures and Papa's yearly almanac calendar. The old wood stove stared at them coldly from the corner. Emptiness dwelt where warmth and laughter had once lived.

On cold winter nights, they'd carry the kerosene lamp upstairs to a tiny bedroom, snug under the eaves. Blowing out their light, they'd snuggle beneath downy covers, nestle their feet to a warm, flannel-wrapped brick, and whisper secrets into the night.

Giggles, whispers, and shared secrets echoed like a haunting refrain throughout the stuffy rooms filled with old mattresses, discarded furniture, and refuse.

"Must be the maid's day off," Josie muttered.

"Hush," Elza retorted as she brushed a cobweb from her face and struggled to open the window that let in God's air-conditioning.

They had come to sort and clean. Hours later amidst the litter of bygone days, they found a long-forgotten steamer trunk tucked away in the back of a closet. Inside was the family Bible. Papers, obituaries, yellowed newspaper clippings, and memorabilia were secreted among the musky pages.

Elza smoothed out a brittle piece of news copy. "Look, Josie. Here's a copy of land transfers from the *Weekly Gazette*. Mama must have clipped it. It shows the purchase of this property years ago."

Josie listened as her sister read the notice. It was a link to their heritage, a birthright that had become a responsibility too heavy. She whispered, "And now, it must be sold again."

The sisters hugged each other and shared their grief.

Papa's voice rang through the ages. "It's time to move on, girls. Idle hands are the devil's workshop!"

Clutching their remembrances close, they left home for the last time. Gazing at the Home Place, they memorized each familiar spot.

How could they give it up?

"Every time I look at the back porch, I can see Mama and Papa waving goodbye," Elza remembered.

"Every time I look at the back porch, I see them waiting for me to get home. Many's the time I missed curfew, tried to sneak in, and met them on the back porch." Josie grinned.

Shading their eyes, they looked once more toward the house.

The last rays of sunlight shimmered on the back porch, highlighting the images of the aged couple waving goodbye. Down through the years, they had waved them off to school, off to dates, off to marriage.

They had welcomed them back to wave once more to grandchildren, great-grandchildren, family, and friends. Until, one day, they waved no more.

Now, in a mirage of sunlight and wistfulness of the heart, they were resurrected!

Home is where the heart is, daughters. The sticks and stones of this old place will become home to others, but precious memories will always return you to your Home Place.

In the never-ending gesture of goodbye, their parents turned and disappeared into the sunlight. ⁓

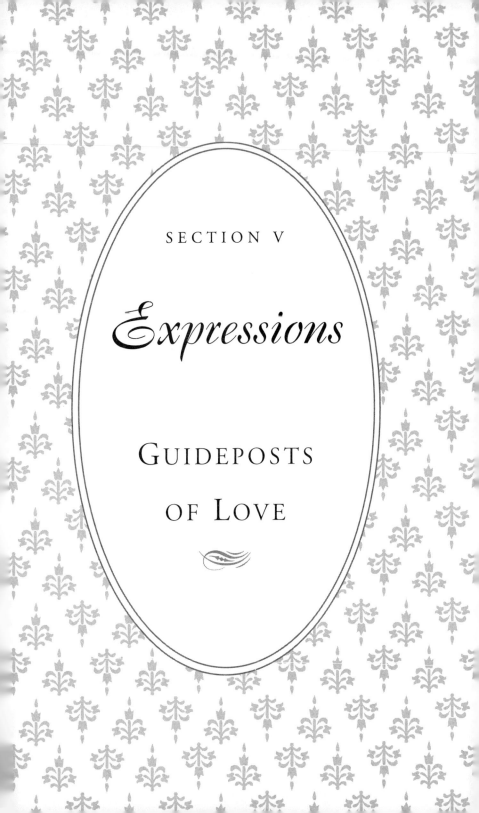

SECTION V

Expressions

GUIDEPOSTS

OF LOVE

M IS FOR . . .

M-m-m is one of baby's first sounds. Can you think of a maternal word that doesn't start with M? M is for . . . Mama, Mother, Mommie, Ma, Mater, Mom, Memaw, Mum . . .

I call her_____ because_____
_____
_____.

No matter what you call her
You know she'll be there.
Because . . .
You're her special creation
Made with loving care. ⌣

LOOKS YOU DON'T LEARN FROM BOOKS!

*T*elecommunication is conveying information without speaking. It's a lot like silent messages that travel between a mother and her offspring, using body language or guttural consonants. If reprimand is intended and said child is within reaching distance, the message is sometimes emphasized with a nudge, poke, or possibly a pinch.

Public gathering places are breeding grounds for these looks. PTA meetings, church meetings, social gatherings, movies, and funerals are places where the rule reigns: children should be seen and not heard.

Raise your hand if your mom is a member of the wait-until-I- get-you-home club.

Her steely-eyed glares can freeze children to their seats.

Her raised eyebrows can ask a question without uttering a word.

A smile can be deceiving if the eyes don't cooperate.

A slight shake of the head, accented with a dainty frown, is the beginning of the end if not acknowledged.

The soft clearing of her throat is a warning to look at her for further instructions.

A nudge, a frown, and a slight rub of the nose could mean one of many things: Quit digging in your nose for boogers; your nose is running; wipe your nose; or was that you who passed gas? If so, don't do it again. It's up to you to figure out which one.

When asking permission to do something, although Mom smiles and seemingly gives her approval, beware if she squeezes your arm, hand, or shoulder in a negative way. *Bow out or wait until she gets you home.*

Be alert for a quick whisper, a directive nudge, or a swift kick under the table when dinner manners are a problem.

If you've received something and hear her clearing her throat, it's a sure sign you've forgotten to say, "Thank you."

Even when you're grown, married, and have children of your own and are directing them with your own body language of reprimand, you should still be alert for your mom's instructions. Remember, no matter what lofty age you've achieved, your mother's telecommunication can veto yours. Age does have its advantages, so remember it! You may not have to worry about *wait until I get you home anymore,* but any mom worth her weight in silent communication can still lay a powerful guilt trip whammy on a wayward child. ⌒

CAN YOU SAY IT BETTER?

*S*tores are filled with rows of generic cards proclaiming sentiments for mothers. Have you ever thought you could say it better?

You probably could, but would you?

Probably not, or you wouldn't have been looking. It sounds easy until you try to put your feelings on paper.

I did an online survey, asking people these three questions:

1. Describe a mother. It doesn't have to be your mother, but *a* mother.
2. What would you expect to find in a book for mothers?
3. If God described a mother, what do you think He would say?

Try it! Get some paper and pencil and jot down your answers. Take these thoughts and create your own card and then, the next time you want to give your mother a card, you won't have to go to the store!

Now, enjoy random lines from my online survey describing a mother. ~

WATERMARK MEMORIES OF MOTHER

*C*ares for others before herself."

"Someone who also has to play the role of your father when your dad dies prematurely."

"The sparkle in your eyes that never dies! Because she is that sparkle."

"A woman who had complete faith in her children."

"She doesn't laugh at my embarrassing moments, she cries with me when I need it, she provides me insight and advice, and she sometimes asks for mine."

"As a child, you try everything to not be like her; as an adult, you find yourself doing things like your mother; and as you get older, you hope you have turned out like your mother!"

"A mother is a friend."

"A mother is someone who teaches right from wrong, how to tie shoes, how to face a bully, and how to say thank you."

"A mother is someone who is loving and caring in all ways, yet holds high ideals for her children."

"Being supportive, loving, caring, and happy."

"A mother is far more than the term 'homemaker'; she is, in fact, the architect for that home."

"Instilling in all of her children a confidence to do whatever we set our minds to."

"A female parent is the biological DNA-blood giver to a baby."

"A mother is the woman who must be adored throughout one's lifetime for the gift of sharing how to live life."

"Someone who is concerned, not only for the here and now for her children, but even more so for the hereafter, and does everything in her power to lead them to God."

"A mother should know her children, I mean KNOW her children. If she does, if she's spent a lifetime doing so, she's a mother."

"Caring."

"Pulling out a pan of warm, hot brownies from the oven just as we jumped off of the school bus. We ate all of the hot, moist goodies before we went out to do the evening chores."

"Picnics in the park, laughter, big pancakes, favorite mom on the street."

"Always thinking of others over herself."

"Reed slim with strong arms from dead lifting a four-year-old, a two-year-old, and a new baby."

"She was our confident, our doctor, and the person we went to when worried, hurt, or in trouble. She could be tender, loving, sympathetic, and forgiving, but tough and immovable as needed in discipline enforcement."

"She will pray to heaven and battle anyone or anything on earth for the sake of her children."

"She is part of what makes me whole and who has made me what I am."

"If they bear children, they may be able to care for them. If they do not bear children, they may want to care for other children, still being called 'Mother.'" ⌒

HUMOROUS SENTIMENTS

*M*y sister-in-law's answer to the survey was a reminder to me of the only poem she ever wrote to her mother for a Mother's Day card.

Imagine her mom's face when she read this!

M is for the mud flaps on your pickup.
O is for the odor from your arm.
T is for the tattoos we won't mention.
H is for the haze from your cigar.
E is for enormous—that's your bottom.
R is for the reject that you are.

Put them all together, they spell MOTHER.
You'll find her down at Frankie's, at the bar.

By Georgia Hale, from her head. ∼

EXPRESSIVE CURES, SOLUTIONS, SAYINGS, AND ADVICE

*T*hose soothing words "Let me kiss it and make it well!" surely reduced the sale of medicine around the world. The next best thing to mom's kiss on an "ouchie" was the treat promised if you didn't cry. The badge of honor was the Band-Aid she placed on the ouchie.

Mothers accumulate an amazing amount of remedies for ouchies. You'd do well to copy your mother's list for future reference.

Here is a sampling of the love mothers shared over the years and a few of the anecdotes my mother's sisters passed along to me.

KINFOLK CURES

Splinters can be removed with scotch tape; if that fails, tweezers or a needle can be used for extraction.

Butter is good to put on a burn.

Hairspray will keep flying insects away from you.

Water/baking soda mixture will take the sting out of a wasp bite.

Blowing smoke in ears is good for an earache.

KINFOLK SOLUTIONS

Mother's sister, Molly, passed this information along from their growing up years:

Mom (this was my grandmother) didn't have a washing machine when we were growing up. We would heat water in a big iron pot in the yard and get some washtubs and separate our whites from colored clothes. We'd get out her homemade lye soap and rub boards. Soon all our dirty clothes would be clean, rinsed, and hanging on the clotheslines out in the fresh air to dry.

Our yard didn't have any grass. Mom would get several brooms and say to us children, "Let's sweep the yard and get it all cleaned up."

We children would all go to the field to hoe the crops or to pick the cotton. We would find a ripe watermelon, and we'd all stop and cut it open and sit down on our cotton sacks and have a watermelon feast.

We children and Mom would go swimming in the creek.

We'd help Mom gather and can plums, pears, and the vegetables we'd planted—corn, green beans, and black-eyed peas. Mom showed us how to make grape jelly from possum grapes.

Aunt Joyce added this "solution" to the childhood recollections:
Mother tied bread wrappers around my shoes before I walked to school to keep my feet warm.

KINFOLK SAYINGS
A watched pot never boils.

Be a task both great or small
    Do it well, or not at all.

A still tongue makes a wise head.

A bird in the hand is worth two in the bush.

A rolling stone gathers no moss.

The grass is always greener on the other side of the fence.

Don't change horses in the middle of the stream.

Don't put the cart before the horse.

There ain't no flies on me.

Ignorance is bliss, but only to the ignorant.

He took a shot in the dark.

A woman, a dog, and a walnut tree,
        The more you beat 'em, the better they be.

If you can't take the heat, get out of the kitchen.

It will all come out in the wash.

Two heads are better than one.

Beauty is only skin deep,
        ugly is to the bone.
Beauty fades away
        but ugly holds its own.

Even an old dish towel is pretty if it's clean.

Waste not, want not.

It's better to be thought a fool
> than to open one's mouth and
> remove all doubt.

People are like wheelbarrows,
> useful only when pushed
> and very easily upset.

The electrical age is wonderful.
> Everything in the house is controlled
> by switches except the children.

Most of the trouble we have comes from saying yes too soon and
> no too late.

KINFOLK ADVICE

This advice was also passed on to me by Aunt Molly in her own words:

Mama encouraged all of us children to get an education. She started us young and helped us learn everything she could for as long as she could. ⌒

THE WAY TO THE FAMILY'S HEARTS IS THROUGH THEIR STOMACHS

*G*randma had a lot of good recipes. The recipe was not always on paper but in her head or *by heart*. My grandma could cook up a meal from almost nothing.

We would be wondering what we were going to have to eat and, all of a sudden, Grandma would have a good meal on the table. Today, most women have to go to the grocery store before they can even start to prepare a meal.

Cooking is an expression of love. I asked relatives to tell me recipes so I could write them down. Grandma's original portions of measurements were impossible to translate: a pinch of this, a tad of that, a smidgeon here, and a sprinkle there.

Each generation of family has revised the portions to suit its needs, but we will remember with fondness when anyone asked Grandma how she knew if her portions were right, her answer was always the same, "Taste it!"

You are invited to "taste" some of my family's favorite recipes.

AFTER SCHOOL TEA CAKES

1 cup flour	1/4 cup butter (softened)
3/4 cup sugar	1/2 teaspoon salt
1 egg	1/2 cup milk
2 teaspoons baking powder	

Heat oven to 350 degrees.
Sift together flour, baking powder and salt. Set aside.
In a medium bowl, beat egg. Mix in butter and milk.
Sift dry ingredients into mixture. Blend mixture into a dough.
Roll dough out on a cutting board. Use a biscuit cutter to cut the tea cakes. Place them on a greased cookie sheet. Bake 10 to 12 minutes or until slightly brown. While still warm, roll them in granulated sugar.

MAMIE'S DUMPLINGS

8 eggs	1 teaspoon baking powder
8 teaspoons shortening (level)	2 quarts chicken broth.
8 tablespoons cream	Black pepper

Bring chicken broth to a boil.
Lower burner to simmer.
Beat eggs and mix with shortening and cream.
Sift flour and baking powder in a little at a time
to make a stiff dough.
Knead the dough like biscuit dough.
Roll out. Cut in strips.
Lay strips out on wax paper to dry until stiff.
Pinch off pieces and drop a few at a time into the hot broth.
Cook covered until tender.
Pepper to taste and serve.

MOM'S ICEBOX COOKIES

1 cup butter	1/2 teaspoon soda
2 cups brown sugar	1/2 teaspoon cream of tartar
3 small eggs	3 cups flour
1/2 teaspoon vanilla	1 cup nuts (walnuts or pecans)

In a large bowl, mix sugar, butter, and vanilla together. Beat eggs and add to mixture.

In a separate bowl, sift together flour, soda, and cream of tartar. Add crushed nuts or pecans. Stir into wet ingredients, beating until dough thickens. Mix and mold into a long roll on the molding board. Preferably mix them at night and put them in the refrigerator until morning.

Take out of refrigerator and slice in very thin slices and bake at 350 degrees for 6 to 8 minutes or until light brown. Decorate as you please. Let cool before removing from the pan. This makes approximately 3 dozen cookies.

They are delicious and will keep indefinitely. Fine to take on a trip.

MAMIE'S DATE LOAF

1 box graham crackers
1 small box dates
1 medium package marshmallows, pecans, and coconut
1 cup sweet milk

Chop marshmallows in a large bowl. Add milk. Let stand about one hour. Add pecans, coconut, and chopped dates. Crumble graham crackers and add to mixture until thick enough to roll out. Roll in rest of crumbs. Put in refrigerator. Cut in slices to serve.

—

EASY POPCORN BALLS

 3 quarts popcorn
 1 teaspoon salt
 1 stick margarine or butter
 Large package marshmallows

Pop corn to make 3 quarts. Pour into large pan and add salt to taste. In a medium saucepan put 1 stick of margarine or butter and one large package of marshmallows. Place over low flame until melted. Pour over popped corn and stir until coated. Grease hands and shape into balls.
Nuts may be added, if desired.

CHRISTMAS WASSAIL TEA

This tea is delicious to serve for the holidays and fills the house with a delectable aroma.

 6 cinnamon sticks
 3 oranges
 16 whole cloves
 6 cups apple juice or cider
 1 pint (2 cups) cranberry juice cocktail
 1/4 cup sugar
 1 teaspoon aromatic bitters
 1 cup rum

Stud 3 oranges with 16 whole cloves.
Put in a cheesecloth bag with cinnamon sticks. Lay in a pan large enough to hold the apple juice or cider and cranberry juice cocktail. Add sugar and aromatic bitters.
Cook over low flame covered. Simmer 10 minutes. Remove cheesecloth bag with fruit.
Add 1 cup rum. Serve. Or store in refrigerator when cool.
Reheat before serving if stored.

MAMIE'S GINGERBREAD

2 1/4 cups flour	1 egg
1/3 cup sugar	1 teaspoon soda
1 teaspoon molasses	1 teaspoon ginger
3/4 cup hot water	1 teaspoon cinnamon
1/2 cup shortening	3/4 teaspoon salt

In a large bowl beat egg and sugar. Add shortening and mix well. Combine hot water and molasses and add to mixture. Mix for about 4 minutes. Sift together flour, soda, ginger, cinnamon, and salt.
Combine dry ingredients with molasses mixture and mix well. Place in 9x9x2 inch greased pan. Bake at 350 degrees for 35 minutes. Serve warm, plain, or with whipped cream.

AUNT NORMA'S
UNCOOKED GREEN TOMATO RELISH

2 small heads cabbage
8 carrots
1 gallon green tomatoes
5 red mango peppers
4 hot peppers
3 pints vinegar
1/2 cup salt
6 cups sugar
2 teaspoons celery seed

Grind all the vegetables and sprinkle with salt. Let stand 1 or 2 hours. Drain and add vinegar, sugar, and celery seed. Mix well (DO NOT COOK) Put in sterilized jars and seal for storage.

FRESH STRAWBERRY PIE

1 quart strawberries, sliced,
    keep a few whole berries to decorate

1 cup strawberry juice	1/8 teaspoon salt
7/8 cup sugar	1 can whipped topping
3 tablespoons cornstarch	Prepared pie crust (store-bought)

Bake prepared pie crust according to directions. Cool and have ready.

Mix together juice, sugar, cornstarch, and salt in a large pan. Cook on top of stove until it is thick and clear. Cool. When mixture is congealed, mix with 1 quart sliced strawberries. Reserve a few whole berries. Pour mixture into baked pie crust. Chill in refrigerator. Serve with whipped topping. Decorate with whole berries. Serves 6.

CORN BREAD SALAD

1 pan corn bread or 2 packages of Jiffy corn bread mix,
    prepared and baked.

1 medium onion, diced

3 stalks celery, diced

1 large green pepper, diced

1 large tomato, diced

1 dozen hard-boiled eggs, 11 diced & 1 sliced

1 8-ounce jar real mayonnaise

1 teaspoon salt

Crumble corn bread into a large bowl. Mix together onion, celery, green pepper, tomato, and 11 eggs. Save 1 egg for garnish. Combine the mixture with corn bread and mix together with enough mayonnaise to moisten. Garnish with remaining egg, sliced. Serve.

SNOW ICE CREAM

2 eggs
1 cup sugar
1 8-ounce can evaporated milk
1 tablespoon vanilla

Large pan of freshly fallen snow. Clear off top snow and dip freshly fallen, well-packed snow from snow drift.

In a large bowl, beat eggs together with sugar and vanilla. Add can of evaporated milk to the mixture. Stir well.

Add snow slowly to prepared mixture. Stir until desired texture is achieved. Serve immediately.

(If you'd like chocolate ice cream, add 1/2 cup of cocoa to the cup of sugar before adding it to the rest of the mixture.)

JANE'S SEVEN LAYER COOKIES

1 stick butter
1 1/2 cups graham cracker crumbs
1 6-ounce bag chocolate chips
1 6-ounce bag butterscotch chips

1 cup crushed walnut goodies
1 cup shredded coconut
1 can Eagle Brand milk

Heat oven to 350 degrees.

Melt one stick butter slowly in saucepan over a low flame, being careful not to burn. Pour butter into a 9x13 baking pan. Add graham cracker crumbs to cover bottom of pan. Then add layer by layer, chocolate chips, crushed nuts, butterscotch chips. Pour coconut over top of layers and pour Eagle Brand milk over the top. Cook for 15-20 minutes or until it begins to brown. Let cool and cut into squares for serving. It can be kept indefinitely if not eaten immediately.

MOM'S SUNSHINE CAKE

Prepare a person-sized container,
The kind sent from up above.
Add a peck of kisses,
Pour in a bushel of love.
Stir in a ton of understanding,
Season with a tablespoon of pride.
Mix a teaspoon of anger with
A gallon of tears you try to hide.
Whip in a handful of spankings,
Numerous sticks of discipline.
Add a pound of consideration,
Increase forbearance to a ton.
Add five pounds of admiration,
Squeeze to shape just right.
Add liberation at separate intervals,
Mix in a dose of worry late at night.
Pour into a tub full of rainbows,
Be prepared to share what you make,
Ice with golden bits of miracles,
Serve Mom's Sunshine Cake.
Serve warm with an armful of hugs,
A box of praise, and then some.
The more you serve, the more you have,
It'll last for years to come.

Various other ingredients can be added for quality. Season to individual taste. Can be stored indefinitely. ∿

Feel Free to Express Yourself

ow long has it been since you read a fairy tale to a child? Yeah, I know, it's easier to watch a video or a television program with them. But often as we begin to watch a television show with a bunch of kids, we realize we should be turning it off because of the content.

Sometimes when we start to switch channels or turn off the television, the children say, "It's not like we haven't seen it before."

As a grandmother, I decided to make a statement. No more violence, sex, and horror. I turned off the television, grabbed up an old-fashioned storybook, and said, "Okay, you guys, I'm going to read you one of my favorite fairy tales. My mom used to read this one to me."

I flipped through the pages. "Okay, listen up. This is the story of a brother and sister named Hansel and Gretel."

The kid said, "Hey, I've read this one. It's about these two little German kids. Come on, you guys, chill out. This one's got some bad scenes in it."

I'm still back on the German part. "How do we know these kids are German?"

"Get real, Grandma. Look at their names, for gosh sakes."

Well, I can live with that. "Okay. Hansel and Gretel's mother died. Their father remarried and they had a stepmother."

"Does it say their mom died? Maybe their old man got a divorce like Timmy's dad. Did you know his mom ran off and left them?"

"Uh, no. The book doesn't actually say their mom died. I never questioned it. I just assumed she died."

"Hey, you need to get the facts straight. Never assume. If you assume, it makes an <u>ass</u> outta <u>u</u> and <u>me</u>."

"All right, already. Whatever. Hansel and Gretel live with their dad and their wicked stepmother, okay?"

"Can we name the wicked stepmother Charlotte? My friend, Nancy, has a wicked stepmother. Well, Nancy's wicked stepmother is not actually married to Nancy's dad. She's more like a wicked live-in, but her name is Aunt Charlotte."

"Yeah, all right. We'll call Hansel and Gretel's wicked live-in stepmother Aunt Charlotte. Now, are you satisfied, can we get on with the story?"

"Chill out, Grandma. It was your idea to read this dumb story. We're just trying to bring it in focus."

"Well, focus on this and listen. Aunt Charlotte didn't want to share her new hubby with two kids by his former marriage. So, she gave him a choice. "Romeo, it's them or me.""

No comment.

I guess I am finally speaking the "now" language. I don't remember this fairy tale being so complicated.

"Hansel and Gretel's dad asked his bride, er, live-in, 'What will I do with the children?'"

"Hey, listen to this, you guys. It's like something out of *Hand That Rocks The Cradle,* that old video we rented the other night. Remember, the old -itch tells him to lose them in the woods," the kid says.

"Hey! Pardon me! That's witch and she doesn't come along until later in the story. Now, pipe down. I'm telling the story."

"Sorry, Grandma, I was just trying to move it along a little faster. Them dudes haven't even got to the woods yet."

"When Hansel and Gretel's dad asked Aunt Charlotte what to do with the children after she's given him a choice between her and them, she tells him to take them into the woods and leave them."

"And their dad says they'll starve, right?" the kid says.

"Right. And, wicked person that Aunt Charlotte is, she answers, 'So be it.'"

The kid breaks in, "Poor old Dad. Looks like he's caught between a rock and a hard place. But, he steals some bread outta Aunt

Charlotte's breadbox and gives it to his kids who he's about to leave in the forest to die. Guess he wanted to show that broad who wears the pants in his family."

"Jeez! Do you want to tell the story? Or do you want me to continue?"

"I thought you'd never ask, Grandma. I'll do the honors. The next morning Pops takes his kids for a walk in the woods and gives them their bread. Good thing the kids have been eavesdropping. Hansel whispers to his sister to save her bread, and he'll leave a trail of bread crumbs so they can find their way back home."

I settle back with the rest of the gang to listen as the story unwinds. If you can't beat them, join them, I always say.

Taking a deep breath, the kid continues, "Wouldn't you know, after their old man ditches them, they hunt for the trail of crumbs. Some dumb greedy birds have eaten the bread. Hansel and Gretel are really lost in the deep dark forest as their dad returns home for a second honeymoon."

The kid has run out of breath, so I take over, "What to do? Gretel offers to share her bread. They eat and soon fall asleep under a tree. But, God looks after children. No bad forest animals eat them. The next morning they awake to a new adventure. Hansel takes his sister by the hand and they try to find their way home. They wander deeper and deeper into the forest. Soon they come to a pretty little cottage."

The kid jumps back in and continues the story, "Nice cottage. Neat fence, cool yard, awesome house, piece of cake! Or was it gingerbread? Whatever, it was better than the store-bought bread Aunt Charlotte didn't bake."

The kid stops and winks in my direction, then hurries on, "Forgetting the manners their dear, little mama had taught them, they enter the yard and begin helping themselves to some of the siding and shingles of gingerbread.

"The old witch says, 'What's that I hear? Sounds like termites. I'd better call Orkin.' The old witch's hearing is better than her eyesight.

You'll find out as the story progresses. Following the munching sounds, Witch Hazel discovers two overgrown termites, Hansel and Gretel.

"Looks like some good eating to me, she thinks. *But, I need the girl to help me in the kitchen. We'll fatten the boy up to eat."*

The kid stops suddenly and yells, "Boo!"

The children all scream.

He continues, "So Witch Hazel puts Gretel to work and Hansel into a cage. Personally, Gretel would have rather been the go-go dancer in the cage—until she found out the real reason her brother was hanging around."

The kid gives a bad imitation of Gretel, "You're going to what? Eat Hansel? I beg your pardon, he's one skinny kid. Just a stick, no meat on his bones.

"So, the old witch gives Gretel food to fatten up Hansel. They share the food while the old witch is busy heating up her ovens. She can't see good, guess she lost her contacts. Dumb broad crawls into the oven to check it out. Then she comes over and demands Hansel stick out his finger so she can see how much weight he's gained."

The kid pauses dramatically, he grins and extends his middle finger and says, "So Hansel gives the old witch the finger."

The kids all break up laughing. I don't even try to straighten them out. This fairy tale is almost over, I hope. "Get on with it or do you want me to finish?"

"Nah, Grandma, I've come this far. I'll close. Hansel don't give the old witch his real finger. He puts out a stick Gretel has given him. When Witch Hazel takes hold of the stick and feels how skinny Hansel is, she goes into a trance.

"The old witch wanders back over to the oven and sticks her head in. Gretel lets her brother outta the cage and they go push the old witch into the oven and close the door. Then they run away back into the forest where a forest ranger finds them.

"The ranger says he smelled smoke and asks if they're trying to burn down the forest.

"They tell him no, they're just trying to brew up some healing tonic by burning Witch Hazel!"

I wondered why the kid had named the witch "Hazel." Now I'm glad I didn't ask.

The kid, disappointed in my reaction or lack of it says, "The ranger gets the joke and laughs."

The kid stops and looks around. None of the kids get the joke. I do, but act like I don't. Why encourage him?

He hurriedly ends the fairy tale, "So the ranger takes the children back home. Dad's live-in has left him for a younger guy, and he welcomes the kids back with open arms. The end."

The children get up and migrate back to the television and switch it on.

"Hey, Grandma, lookit! They're showing a re-run of *Liar, Liar.* In case you haven't seen it, this dude tells lies and it gets him in all kind of trouble."

"Sounds like Pinocchio! Does his nose grow when he tells a lie?"

The kid grins, "No, but he gets in a whale of a lot of trouble."

"Scoot over," I say as I push onto the sofa, "I always like a Jim Carrey movie."

"Now you're talking, Grandma!" ⌒

THAT'S WHAT KEEPS ME GOING

When Mom married Dad, she left her home state. She brought with her a heart full of love. Sharing hugs and kisses was her family's way of showing affection.

Mom soon found her new husband's family expressed their love in a less emotional way and were not outwardly demonstrative.

Being raised in Dad's home state, we mimicked his family's inhibited ways. My brother and I learned love nurtured but didn't surpass the boundaries of joyful emotion. We never doubted we were loved—we just didn't talk about it or show it much. It was there, deep down, waiting for a special moment.

When we visited Mom's family, we were greeted with . . . Hugs! Kisses! They actually said, aloud, "I love you!" Soon we were hugging and kissing, along with the rest of Mom's family. Then we returned home and resumed our pattern of polite restraint.

My brother and I were still in elementary school when Mom attended a Pentecostal revival and found salvation. While Dad watched from the sidelines, gospel religion claimed his family. My brother and I, along with our mom, were baptized in a creek and joined the Freewill Baptist Church.

God's love was an emotional experience for Mom. Clapping, shouting, and singing lively church hymns were ways she praised her Lord. My brother's and my wide-eyed acceptance of this religion was less expressive, but not less heartfelt.

Dad's acceptance of the Lord as his savior was a personal experience conducted quietly at a revival one evening at the First Baptist Church.

Mom's Christian influence on friends, neighbors, and family was a living testimony.

A custom we shared with others at church was the giving of corsages on Mother's Day. Tradition dictated a mother wore red flowers if her mother was living, white flowers if her mother was dead.

Mom was appreciative of her corsage, but preferred flowers in their natural habitat. Her yard and garden were the envy of our neighborhood.

After Dad's death, Mom's world revolved around her children, her grandchildren, and her church. She shared an emotional love with her grandchildren. When they exchanged hugs and kisses, she'd say, "That's what keeps me going, knowing someone cares."

I yearned to be included in their hugs and kisses, but a lifetime of sharing affection the way Dad's family did could not be easily altered. Yet, as I assumed the role of mother and my mom became the grandma, I learned the special meaning of knowing someone cares through my children's hugs and kisses.

Friendship was a bonus that slipped into my relationship with Mom as she guided me through paths she had already traveled.

We brought back a mimosa tree from Mom's home state and transplanted it in my backyard. The tree produced abundant foliage but, despite our efforts, it never bloomed with the fragile, lovely flowers for which it was known.

Mom said, "My home state is having a little trouble transplanting to your dad's native soil. It took me awhile to adjust too. Have faith, one day it'll bloom."

Too soon Mom became ill and our relationship changed. She became childlike. My brother and I assumed the parenting role. Chaste walls came tumbling down. We learned to share our love through hugs and kisses. Saying the words "I love you" was easy when we remembered her words, "That's what keeps me going . . ."

Mom was eighty years old when she died. We could not wish her back to this world of suffering but sought reassurance in divine hope.

The next Mother's Day, for the first time, I wore a white corsage. As a family, we shared hugs and kisses, remembering a mother and grandma who believed, "That's what keeps you going . . ."

Later, I pulled Mom's Bible from my bookcase by the window and leafed through its well-worn pages, pausing to read little notes she'd tucked inside. Among them was her favorite scripture, Philippians 4:11: "Not that I speak in respect of want; for I have learned, in whatsoever state I am, therewith to be content."

Tears blurred my vision as I stared out the window at our mimosa tree.

"Mom," I whispered.

Lush with foliage, the tree swayed in the breeze. Nestled near the crest was a single, lovely white bloom: a corsage pinned upon its lapel. ⌢

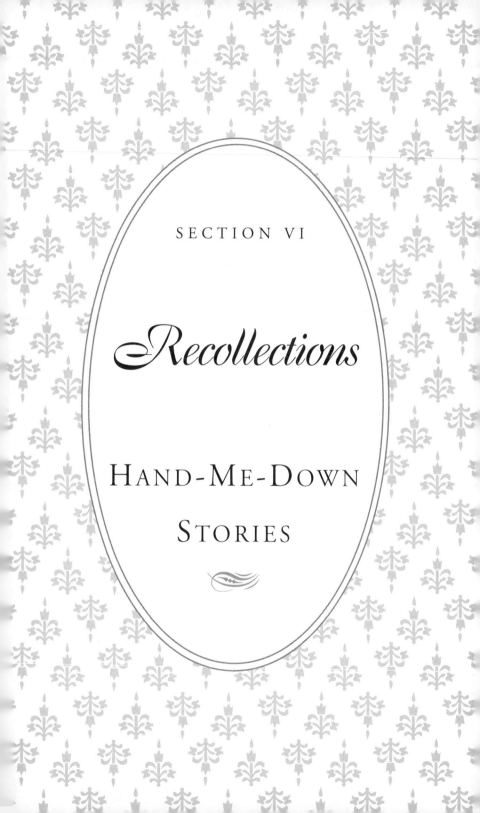

SECTION VI

Recollections

HAND-ME-DOWN
STORIES

GLAMOUR HAS ITS PRICE

I spent precious childhood hours sitting on a stool in front of Mom while she fashioned my fat Shirley Temple curls.

Shirley was always Mom's ideal, but as I grew older, I chose another movie star to impersonate: Liz Taylor. Mom and I leafed through magazines looking at hairstyles. We saw pigtails, pompadours and bangs. If only I'd inherited Mom's naturally curly hair, I could have puffed my hair out like Liz.

Then I discovered a place called a *beauty shop.*

One day I came home from school with an exciting tale about a friend who had been to the beauty shop and had a *permanent wave.* "Honest, Mom, her hair had curls that stayed in place. No rolling or combing out. She said she just runs a brush through it each day."

Mom must have quizzed her friends concerning permanent waves. She passed along horror stories about electric attachments and burned curls.

It didn't faze me. I continued my crusade to have a permanent wave. I even enlisted Dad's help. Finally we wore Mom down as Dad teased her about believing gossip.

As Mom and I walked to the beauty shop, I knew in my heart it was the answer to all the time spent on my hair.

We took a seat in the beauty shop to wait our turn. I watched a girl leaning back in a chair while the Beauty Shop Woman washed her hair. I saw a lady getting her hair rolled. I peered at a woman whose head was covered with a hood, which had to be a dryer.

Then, in a corner I saw what looked like an electric chair in the death house. It had strings of cords hanging from the top with a metal deal at the end of each one.

"Jane Shewmaker!" It was my turn to become instantly beautiful.

Washed, dried, and ready for my permanent wave, I reluctantly approached the electric chair. The Beauty Shop Woman seated me beneath the dangling wires and started attaching them to my head. I glanced at Mom and saw her brush at her cheek. *Was she crying?*

When I was completely hooked up, the Beauty Shop Woman plugged in the machine, warning it might get a little hot.

She smiled, "But . . . that's the price we pay for permanent curls, Jane."

She was right. It got hot. Finally, she unplugged me and started to detach the curlers.

I heard Mom gasp. I looked at her and she was crying in earnest.

I looked at the Beauty Shop Woman for an answer and found it lying in her hand: *one of my Shirley Temple curls.*

Oh, my gosh! The stories were all true. My hair had been burned from my head. I started crying.

The Beauty Shop Woman stuttered, "I've never had this happen before."

She looked at me as if I'd caused my hair to come out.

I felt guilty. But, to save my curls, I couldn't think of anything I'd done bad enough to cause me to be bald at this early age.

The lady rushed me to her chair, turned me away from the mirror, and started to brush my hair. When she had finished, she turned me to face the mirror.

My hair was beautiful! I looked like a movie star. My hands moved toward the bald spot.

"Don't mess your pretty curls, Jane," the Beauty Shop Woman warned.

Mom opened her purse to pay her. My mother, who was the most gracious woman I knew, used a tone of voice on the Beauty Shop Woman that I heard only when I was in bad trouble. I knew Mom was mad.

The Beauty Shop Woman knew it too. "Mrs. Shewmaker, I'm not

going to charge you full price for Janie's permanent wave. I'm so sorry. I don't know what happened, but the hair will grow out and the permanent wave gave Jane's hair body so it covers the spot beautifully."

Mom glared at the Beauty Shop Woman, pushed the money toward her, grabbed me by the hand, and started to the door.

"Jane," the Beauty Shop Woman called after us.

I turned.

"Do you like ice cream?"

I stared at her. *Do dogs chase rabbits?*

"Here's some money, I want to treat you to some ice cream." She extended her hand to me.

I reached toward her.

Mom jerked me.

I looked at Mom.

Mom was smiling her *don't you dare* smile. She turned it on the Beauty Shop Woman, who froze in her tracks. "No, thank you."

We were out the door and on the sidewalk before I could say *ice cream*.

Mom stomped along the street, headed toward Dad's garage.

Trouble was brewing. Mom seldom bothered Dad during business hours unless it was an emergency.

Inside Dad's filling station, he and some of his cronies stood visiting. We must have entered after a particularly good joke because the place filled with laughter.

Mom looked embarrassed and pulled me in front of her. I felt as if I were the cause of the laughter. My hand moved toward my head. Was my bald spot showing?

The men turned to greet us, "Hello, Mrs. Shewmaker. And, Blaine, is this your daughter, Jane, all grown-up? She's a young Elizabeth Taylor. What lovely hair she has."

Mom gasped.

Dad looked at Mom. Then he turned to me.

I guess I still had a grin pasted on from the compliment I'd just received and the relief that I wasn't the source of the men's laughter.

Dad ran his hand over my shining mass of permanent wave. "Jane, your hair looks fine."

He turned to Mom and said, "See, Nez, you were frightened for nothing." He turned to his friends. "Nez thought if she took Jane to the beauty shop, they'd burn her curls off. Isn't that a hoot?" He joined the men as they laughed again.

Mom pulled me toward the door. As we started out, she mumbled something that sounded like, "Men! They probably would have taken the Judas's ice cream money too."

I turned to look at Dad. He raised his eyebrows in question.

I raised mine and grinned a *I'll tell you later.*

Mom and I walked home in silence.

I wondered if Shirley Temple and Liz Taylor paid such a high price for glamour. Could they have bald spots beneath their lovely hairdos?

It was a hot day. Ice cream sure would have tasted good, but I knew better than to suggest it. ⌣

HEROINES COME IN ALL SIZES, SHAPES, AND FANS

*T*his book's not bigger than a minute."

My cousin, Sherry, and I took turns thumbing through the picture book we'd found upstairs in our grandparents' attic. It was almost like a movie if you flipped the pages fast enough. And, the picture on the front! Woo! Woo!

"Who is this lady?" Sherry peered closer at the curvaceous blonde who was wearing nothing but two large feather fans and fancy high heel slippers.

I grabbed the book. "Let me see!" I stared hard at the blonde. "Is it Betty Grable?"

Sherry shook her head. "She's got pretty legs, but I don't think they're worth a million dollars."

"My dad said Fox Studio only insured her legs for a quarter million dollars."

"Only a mere quarter million?" Sherry said in a haughty voice.

We burst out laughing. We spent the next half hour trying to decided if either one of us might have legs that would require insurance with Lloyds of London some day. By the time our grandma came hunting for us, we had talked our way through Betty's first husband, Jackie Coogan, the former child star, and had progressed to her current husband, Band Leader Harry James.

Sherry imitated Betty Grable's famous pinup pose. "I'm Betty Grable, darling! My picture adorned G.I. barracks all over the world during World War II."

I tried to copy her stance. "I'm 'what's her name' in the book and I bet my picture was in a few barracks too!"

The sound of applause resounded from the stairwell where

Grandma had been watching.

Embarrassed, we plopped down on the floor, red faced.

I flipped through the pages of the little book. "Who is this lady?"

Grandma took the book from my hand and did some flipping of her own. Smiling, she said an odd thing. "Our families claim to fame is as perilous as a feather in one of Cousin Sally's fans."

"Who's Cousin Sally?" we chorused.

Grandma continued in a hushed voice that caused us to huddle closer to her. "Sally Rand is a famous fan dancer. She happens to be our kin! Her real name is Helen Gould Beck, and she was born in Hickory County, Missouri."

"Is she kin to Grandma and Grandpa Beck?"

"Why do you think I called her cousin?"

"Tell us about Sally, er, Helen, Grandma."

Grandma sat on the attic floor beside us, holding the book, instinctively flipping the pages to make her cousin Sally move her fans. "Helen's pa was a mail carrier and her ma kept house. Helen never was satisfied to live in a small town. She wanted to be an entertainer. One day she just packed up and took off for Kansas City."

"How old was she?"

"Thirteen and already a beauty. She'd taught herself to use makeup and make the most of her talents."

"Did she become a movie star?"

"Not right away. She came back home and helped her ma and pa with their grocery store for a while. The next thing we knew she was calling herself Sally. She left for New York, where she worked in vaudeville as a chorus girl. Then, we heard she'd joined a traveling troupe. When she finally got to Hollywood, she changed her name from Sally Beck to Sally Rand."

"Then was she in the movies?"

"She did some bit parts in silent films as a supporting actress and finally starred in a leading role. Let's see if I can remember some of her films." Grandma thought a minute. "I think her first one was called

The Texas Bearcat. Later, there was *Getting Gertie's Garter, A Girl in Every Port,* and several others."

Sherry and I looked at each other, both thinking we could hardly wait to get to school and brag about being kin to a movie star.

Grandma continued, "When talkie films came along, Sally lost out. She went back to New York and worked off-Broadway as a dancer in vaudeville and burlesque. Sally finally got top billing as Sally Rand, the Fan Dancer."

"Does she have any clothes on behind the fans?" I was having second thoughts about claiming kin to Sally Rand.

"We heard Sally wears a flesh-colored body suit. She creates an illusion as she plays peek-a-boo with her audience, moving the fans from side to side. She became an overnight success when she did her revealing dance at the Chicago World's Fair in 1934."

"Hey, that's the year I was born! I can't wait to tell Mom and Dad." It was like an omen that our cousin had become a success my birth year.

Grandma smiled. "Honey, your mom and dad already know." She took the little book and placed it back among the souvenirs.

"Grandma, did you ever want to become famous like your cousin Sally?"

"No, I'm more the grandma type." She got up and positioned herself like the picture of Sally with her fans and smiled down at us.

We scrambled up and did some posing too. "Maybe we could all dance together. I bet we'd be good with fans."

Grandma started downstairs with us following. Looking back over her shoulder, she said, "You're my fans. If I had run off to Hollywood, you might not have been here."

Sherry and I agreed we were glad our grandma wasn't the Beck who had become a fan dancer. But, it was exciting to have Sally Rand as part of our family. As we grew older, we followed her career. She danced before the crowned heads of Europe! Sally Rand later appeared in her own theater restaurant at 168 O'Farrell Street in San Francisco.

Fame comes to each of us in different ways. Helen Gould Beck used illusion to fan the flame of success. In her own way, she was our heroine. ⌒

TELE-PHONE, TELE-GRAPH, TELE-GRANDMA

*D*ad's mother, Mamie, loved her soap operas on the radio: Stella Dallas, Lorenzo Jones, and others.

Grandpa was an avid radio news fan. His world revolved around morning, noon, and evening radio news. The farm reports were business for him. Beware to anyone who interrupted his time with the newscaster.

Living on the farm, my grandparents' social life was a trip to town on Saturdays if the weather was good. So an important part of their communication with the outside world was their telephone.

Their phone was a box-like structure, which hung on the wall in the kitchen, the hub of their home. The box had a protruding mouth-piece and a cone-shaped receiver, which was attached to the box with a cord. A set of bells at the top sounded the warning that someone was calling. If you wanted to call out, you used a crank on the side of the phone.

Most homes shared a party line with several other households. When the phone rang, your call was distinguished by the number of rings or the length of a ring. The operator, or Central, was reached with one long ring, another family with two long rings, and another a long and a short ring. If the phone rang, you knew whether it was for your family or another family on your party line.

Eavesdropping was discouraged, but you lifted your receiver before dialing out in case there was someone on your line.

Mamie said if you picked up the phone and heard voices, it was only polite to listen a moment to see who was talking. You could generally gauge the time the phone would be in use by knowing who was on the phone.

For instance, if Grandpa needed the phone, he was impatient. He would make his call, state his business, and get off the line. Mamie assumed most men did the same. So, if she raised the receiver and heard male voices, she would hang up and wait a few minutes and try again. Most of the time the line would be available.

Mamie hated for someone to pick up while *she* was on the phone talking. She could always tell when someone picked up while on line because she would hear a click.

If that happened to Mamie, she'd raise her voice and say, "Please get off the phone. This is a private conversation."

When she heard the click of hanging up, she'd continue her conversation, finish, and hang up.

But, if Mamie raised the receiver and heard female voices, it was another story. She wouldn't hang up because she said if you hung up, you might never get the line again. Instead, she'd be still and listen, hoping the women were at the end of their conversation.

Mamie would lean against the wall, receiver in hand, listening intently. She claimed she wasn't eavesdropping—she was only waiting. She said it was hard to not listen while you were waiting. Sometimes she would hold her hand over the mouthpiece and chuckle or shake her head in disbelief.

Later, Grandpa would demand to know about the conversation.

Mamie would tease him. "You should never repeat phone conversations."

Mamie knew Grandpa would keep pestering her, so she'd tell him the interesting parts just as he passed along tidbits of overheard gossip to her.

No one was supposed to listen but, as Mamie always said, "Everybody does it. We're only human."

Grandpa hardly ever used the phone unless he had urgent business. He'd raise the receiver to check if the line was free and if he heard women talking and the women were—as he called them—"long-winded," he'd sometimes click the receiver to let them know they'd been tying up the line too long.

If that didn't work, he'd clear his throat and wait. If all else failed and his business couldn't wait, he'd break in and say, "I need the phone line for business."

Usually the ladies would recognize his voice and say, "Excuse me." Then they would terminate their conversation.

Mamie didn't want to be labeled long-winded, so she tried to make her calls short.

Today most people take for granted the use of private telephone lines. Lines are readily available—unless there are teenagers in the family. And now, most homes have more than one phone line, and many have their own cell phones, so party lines are not such a problem.

When Alexander Graham Bell, a Scotsman who invented the telephone in 1876, succeeded in getting his call through on March 10 and spoke these words, "Mr. Watson, come here, I want you!" he opened up a whole new way for the world to express themselves.

Since that fateful day, voices have traveled phone lines to reach out and touch someone. Many depend on e-mail for correspondence since computers have become popular, but in Grandpa and Mamie's day, the phone was a source of entertainment to many.

When Grandpa teased Mamie about listening in on the party line, she answered, "Well, I have my soap operas on the radio and I have my soap operas on the telephone. I sometimes think the ones of the telephone are the best 'cause I know most of the characters personally." ⌒

IDLE HANDS ARE THE DEVIL'S WORKSHOP

*M*amie Shewmaker was the center of her family's universe. She could have been called a genuine professional homemaker.

She could not only raise a chicken to a fryer, but she could wring its neck, cut it up properly, and fry it for Sunday dinner.

The rest of the meal would consist of things she had canned or preserved from her fruit trees, garden, or vines on her surrounding farm. Even the dairy products were from the farm. She milked. The milk was strained for drinking or selling. Cream, which rose to the top, was skimmed for toppings or churned into butter. Buttermilk was derived from the milk.

I thought Mom was fast, but she told me if I walked a day in Mamie's shoes, I would sleep well that night. I tried it one day. It wasn't the walking in her shoes that tired me: it was the movement of her busy body that wore me out.

If Mamie wasn't picking, digging, peeling, kneading, feeding, pulling, or fixing, it must be washday.

Monday was washday. Mamie's only daughter would bring her wash to Mamie's. Mom would go to Mamie's to help and take our family washing. Some of the rest of the family might add to the load, and it became an all-day job.

We're talking about drawing the water from the well, using a rub board and lye soap on the hard stains and work clothes, making starch, and carrying those loads to clothespin them on the outside line to dry. Later, all the clothes had to be taken off the line, carried back in, folded, and distributed to the right piles or placed in Mamie's drawers, linen shelves, or closet.

If this sounds like a full day, it was, especially sandwiched in with all of Mamie's other daily chores. Farm life didn't stop for washday.

It didn't stop for Tuesday's ironing day, either. Cotton was king, and the no-iron days were far ahead. Those starched clothes had to be sprinkled, packed in a basket to keep moist, ironed, and hung on hangers or chairs to dry thoroughly so the starched look would stay. Remember the irons that were kept hot on the stove? Try ironing with those heavy things, and you won't need to lift weights to keep those arm muscles from sagging.

Wednesday, Mamie could heave a sigh of relief that the laundry was finished—until she happened to look into the hamper and see it was already filling up again.

The kitchen was Mamie's domain. If she wasn't kneading bread to set, to rise, to knead out again, she was whipping up a batch of hot biscuits.

The cookstove had to be stoked with wood for the oven to be the right temperature for baking. While it was hot, she might mix up dough for pies, cobblers, or other pastries. Meanwhile, the fillings for those delicacies were bubbling on the stove top, needing to be stirred. The timing was crucial: pie crusts ready; filling ready; egg whites whipped for meringue (the yolks were used in the filling). In addition, a delicate crust braid had to prepared for topping fruit pies.

Never mind the busy work of peeling potatoes, turnips, onions, tomatoes, carrots, or working up batches of fresh green beans, shelling peas, or stemming strawberries.

If the main meal meat wasn't baked in the oven, huge skillets of chicken, ham, beef, pork, duck, or lamb needed to be turned for con-sistency in browning.

Thank God the eggs had been gathered, checked, and stored for the cooking needs or to sell.

The family table was constantly in a state of readiness. A fresh cloth with pepper, salt, toothpicks, and other necessities stood in the center, ready to be set with plates, knives, and forks at a moment's notice. Extra places could be added as needed. Mamie always fixed too much food so visitors could sit down and have plenty.

Mamie's pantry was stocked with any extra food. One of the greatest delights of childhood was to prowl in Mamie's pantry for a snack of leftover cold biscuits, meat, and onions.

Even at the end of the day, if Mamie sat down to glance at her favorite reading, *The Cappers Weekly*, she'd share the jokes or stories with those who wanted to listen.

If the family listened to the radio, Mamie would join them with a bowl of walnuts to be picked out for her cooking needs. If her hands were ever idle, someone might request she peel apples for the group. Did you ever see someone start at the top of the apple and never break the peel as they peeled the whole apple? Mamie did, then she'd quickly cut the apple in fourths, pare the insides on a discarded newspaper, and hand out pieces of apple to those waiting.

She was never too tired to tell stories, share laughter, or get up to find something someone else might have forgotten.

Once I asked, "Mamie, don't your hands ever get tired?"

"Jane, my hands are too busy to get tired. When my hands aren't moving, you'll know I'm dead. Idle hands are the devil's workshop."

Never let it be said that Mamie contributed to the devil's workshop. The only time I can remember seeing Mamie's hands still was when they were folded at last in prayer across her bosom.

And, as I said my last goodbyes, I could almost hear the Lord saying, "Welcome, I can use a hand up here." ⁓

GERONIMO! MAMIE

*M*amie had a large china cabinet filled over the years with gifts from her family of four sons and one daughter. There was always a large box of candy on top of her cabinet. Though I loved candy, as did most of my cousins, we had been warned about asking Mamie for candy.

Instead of asking, we would say, "Mamie, what did you get for Mother's Day?"

Mamie would smile knowingly. "Oh, a box of chocolates. Would you like a piece?"

We'd look innocently at our parents until Mamie persuaded them it was all right. Mamie was our *champion!*

My grandparents lived on a farm. It used to be an overnight trip when they traveled to town to buy farm supplies and sell produce. Their extravagant shopping might come from Sears, Roebuck or Montgomery Ward catalogues. Mamie sewed most of the garments needed to clothe her family.

After Mamie's sons married, she accompanied her daughter or daughters-in-law to Springfield for occasional shopping. My memories of the city are special shopping trips and eating out. It was a treat for Mamie and me.

The south side of the city square was my favorite. The dime stores were islands of paradise. The pastry counters enticed Mamie and me as we prowled, savoring the aroma. After purchasing a bag of donuts, we'd munch as we strolled the square. Mamie said it was a wicked feeling to enjoy eating in public.

My grandmother entered my childhood world so easily, it was hard to believe she belonged to the grown-ups. Like children, we checked out the city square. We swooned over the downtown theater posters and ended up at JCPenney's.

I'll never forget the time Mom and my aunts persuaded Mamie to try on a dress she'd been admiring. When Mamie came out of the dressing room, she was beautiful. Her face glowed as she modeled the dress. My grandmother could have been a movie star that day. The saleslady told her so.

Mamie tossed her head, straightened tired shoulders, and hid her chapped, work-worn hands beneath magically soft folds of the perfect dress as she strutted to the dressing room to try on something more appropriate. She ended up buying a print work dress much like the few hanging in her closet.

As we left, she glanced at the dress. I would have given my whole piggy bank and no shows for a year to buy that dress for Mamie.

I wasn't the only one who shared those feelings. Mamie let out a little squeal when she opened her birthday present from her daughters-in-law and saw the dress. She squeezed back tears as she hugged downy softness to her breast.

Pa asked her where she'd ever wear anything like that dress. She just smiled and hugged it closer. A dress is a fantasy of women. Men seldom look at frills with longing.

I'm sure Pa must have seen a glimpse of the beautiful, young girl he'd married the few times she wore that dress. Or, perhaps he saw her that way every day.

I'm glad Mamie didn't get another box of candy that birthday. I'm glad she got the dress of her dreams, even if it did only hang in her closet.

Now, years later, older—wiser—married with children, I know the secret that made Mamie's face glow that special day. It's nice to have a closet full of work clothes, but it's heaven to have a dream dress hanging in their midst—just in case you ever need it. The fulfillment of soft, silky cloth among the durability of cottons parachutes your fantasies. In your heart, you know you'll never jump, but, just in case . . . Geronimo! Eh, Mamie? ⌒

FUNERAL CLEAN

*C*leanliness is next to godliness. That was the gospel according to Mom.

Her living room was immaculate with everything in its place. Her bedrooms were spic and span. You didn't dare sit on the bed after it was made. I learned that early. I had seen some kids having a fine old time jumping on their beds. I told Mom about it. As if the frown she gave me was not warning enough, she admonished, "The bed is a place to sleep. When it is not being slept in, it is made up, waiting to be slept in. My mother told me, and I'm telling you—do not mess up the bed by jumping on it or sitting on it or doing anything else on it except sleeping."

"Yes, Mom. Sorry I asked, Mom," I said.

"What did you say, young lady?"

"I just said I was sorry I bothered you by asking, Mom."

"Well, change out of your school clothes and be sure to hang them up in your closet."

I was already out of my clothes. They were lying in a pile on the floor. I dashed to the closet, found a hanger, and hung my school dress up in the neat row of dresses Mom had made for me.

One time I had forgotten to change my school dress before I went out to play. I tore it. When I asked my brother what to do, he suggested I hang it up and maybe Mom wouldn't notice. She found that dress, right off, mainly because it was hung up.

I pulled off my school shoes and placed them in the neat row of shoes in the spotless closet. I grabbed my everyday shoes, put them on, and was out the door before Mom could give me another job. If I helped Rex carry in wood, sometimes we'd play basketball.

Later, Mom called, "Rex, Jane, time to come in. You other children better go home. It's time for your supper. Come back tomorrow."

Mom liked for Rex and me to stay in our own yard. Everyone was welcome to come and play. But, when it was time for us to go inside, it was time for them to return to their homes unless we had requested a friend stay for supper or overnight. These invitations had to be arranged ahead of time and checked out with their parents.

Mom was sweeping off her walk where Rex and I had hurriedly swept wood chips out the back door. She had a familiar gleam in her eye.

Rex looked at me. I shook my head. We were both worried. I wasn't about to ask, but we both knew it was about that time because Mom had that *it's almost spring cleaning time* look as she swept.

The good smell of her cooking drew us inside. Her kitchen was spotless. The table was set, waiting for its four diners. Rex and I looked around and wondered what Mom could possibly find to spring clean.

That weekend we found out.

Early Saturday morning, Mom rousted us out and we knew we hadn't misread her "spring cleaning" look. She had a muslin tea towel tied around her dark, naturally curly hair, a dead give-a-way.

"Okay, kids. Rise and shine. It's spring cleaning time. As soon as we have breakfast, we've got a big day ahead of us."

Dad was up and bustling about. He knew what was coming and was hurrying to get out of the house. He gulped his coffee, swallowed his bacon, eggs, and toast almost whole. He stood up, wiped his mouth, smiled in our direction, and winked. Then he picked up his hat, stuck it at a jaunty angle on his head, reached down to peck Mom's cheek, and started for the door.

He almost made it.

"It's early, honey. Don't go just yet. The kids and I are deep cleaning today. I need you to help me with the heavy stuff. Come on, it'll only take a minute to turn the mattresses on our beds. They're too heavy for us."

Rex and I giggled at the pained expression on Dad's face as he followed Mom into the bedroom. He looked back over his shoulder and shrugged.

We smiled and winked.

Before he left, he'd helped turn the mattresses and had carried the heavy rugs out to hang on the line so we could beat the dirt out of them. Finally, after he'd finished moving furniture around in the living room, Dad begged off, saying he was going to be late for work.

I had cleaned the breakfast dishes and cabinets. When Mom came in the kitchen, she put me to scrubbing the stove. Rex got to go out and beat the rugs. Sometimes, if he knew Mom wasn't watching, he'd take his baseball bat and practice his batting swing as he beat the rugs.

That night we were so tired, we welcomed bed. The day had been a nightmare of scrubbing, washing windows, cleaning out the already spotless closets, and re-shining shoes you could already see your reflection in. Each time we thought we were almost finished, Mom would find another spring cleaning chore to do. We even tided up our outdoor toilet.

Saturday night was bath night. Mom warmed water on top of the stove and in the stove reservoir. The washtub was brought in the kitchen, and we took turns taking our weekly bath. Tonight we were filthy. We each ended up with a fresh tub of water.

We settled down in the living room that evening. I snuggled up on my corner of the couch. Just before I dropped off for a nap, I saw Mom standing in the doorway.

Oh, no! I thought. *She's found a job we forgot.* What could it possibly be? We'd even ironed the shoestrings!

"I love the clean smell of our home. Spring cleaning is a big task, and you all did a good job. Our home is *funeral clean.*

"What's funeral clean, Mom?" I muttered.

"Honey, funeral clean is the way I would want my home if I had passed away and friends, family, and neighbors were coming in to pay their respects. Not a speck of dirt in sight." She smiled as she surveyed the room. "Or out of sight."

I smiled and drifted off to sleep. It made me happy to see Mom so pleased with our work.

Every April when the windows look smudged, the kitchen stove feels greasy, and the mattresses need turning, I think of Mom, spring cleaning, and funeral clean.

I look to the heavens and imagine my mom sweeping the golden streets, wiping cobwebs off those pearly gates, and issuing orders as Dad and other family angels fly around, helping Mom spring clean.

I imagine I hear them asking, "When will we be through?"

Dad would reply, "God only knows!"

And Mom would smile as a loud voice booms, "This one's not my call. Cleanliness may be next to godliness, but give that woman a broom, and we'll all learn the meaning of 'A man's work is from sun to sun, but a woman's work is never done.'"

A sudden rain shower washes the earth, clouds slowly drift from the sky, and I bask in the warmth of the sunshine as it glows a little brighter. I believe Mom's smiling because spring cleaning is over for another year, and her world is funeral clean.

As I turn to go inside, a rumble of thunder comes from a distance.

"I know, I know, Mom. I need to do my spring cleaning too." ◠

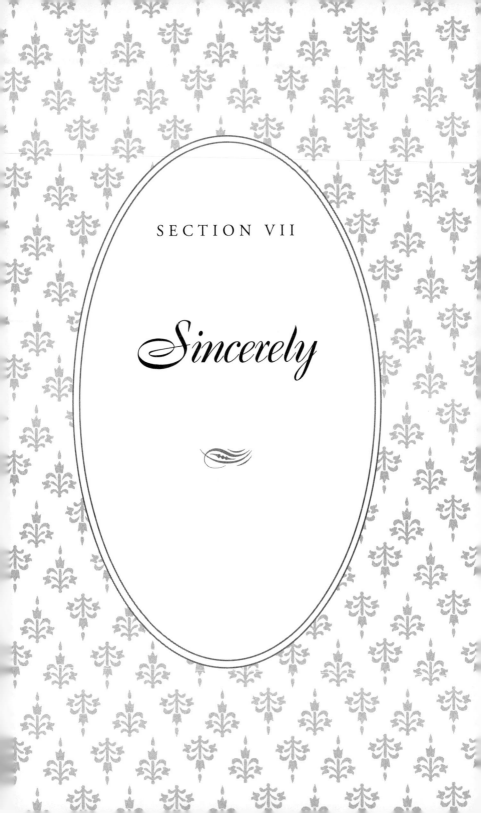

SECTION VII

Sincerely

SINCERELY

*T*his has been quite a journey. Traveling back through childhood days when the word Mother was directed at my mom, into the realm of motherhood—myself, and on through time to become a grandma, ten times blessed. It seems to have happened in the twinkling of an eye.

Each cycle of motherhood holds precious memories. When I was a child, our home was always the gathering place for family and friends. I copied Mom's graciousness and opened our home to relatives and my sons' chums.

As grandma, I remembered kinfolk dinners and festive holidays made for family togetherness and sought to recreate that affectionate closeness.

Following in the footsteps of mothers who have gone before, God willing, one day, I'll move into the next cycle of motherhood and find out how really *great* it can be.

One of Mom's favorite teachings was *turn about is fair play*. With this in mind, I'd like to reveal the secret promised to you at the beginning of this book.

Every Day Is Father's Day is an invitation to revisit our world. This book will show you a different side of our family.

Growing up in Dad's world where a man's word was his bond and a handshake eliminated the need for paperwork, I was privy to "good old boy" talk that should have super-curled my Shirley Temple hairdo.

Daddy's tomboy is taught not to eavesdrop, but when one of his friends says, "When hell freezes over . . . ," I ponder the statement until, one day, I discover the answer in *Every Day Is Father's Day*.

So, if you enjoyed the meal, come on back for dessert! Bring a friend! The proverbial welcome mat is always out, the door is open, and the invitation to come inside and visit is as sincere in the world of literature as the reality of yesterday, today, and tomorrow at the Shewmaker-Hale home.

Sincerely,

Myra Jane Shewmaker Hale

About the Author

Jane Shewmaker Hale is a native of Buffalo, Missouri. She and her husband, Bob, have four sons and ten grandchildren. She is an active partner in their family fireworks business and also Hale Sportswear. Hale was honored in 2001 with her own private fireworks label on which she is pictured as "The Firecracker Lady," a name she is known by to retail customers in the United States. Visit her website, firecrackerlady.com.

Since 1992 she has written an award winning weekly column in *The County Courier*, "Buffalo . . . As I Remember It!" in the voice of her childhood, Little Janie Shewmaker.

She is a freelance photo-journalist having credits with major publications.

Hale is the author of the "Land" series of children's holiday mysteries. Her first four books in the series can be found online at Amazon.com or barnesandnoble.com and in bookstores: *Wonderland*, a Christmas mystery; *Heartland*, a Valentine mystery; *Foreverland*, an Easter myster; and *Boomland*, a 4th of July mystery. *Spookyland*, a Halloween mystery, and *Homeland*, a Thanksgiving mystery, complete the series. Hale owns and operates Rainbow Publications and Toys. She designs and supervises the production of stuffed animals, companions for her books.

Hale is active in many writers groups. She serves on the executive branch of Ozark Writers Inc. and Missouri Writers Guild.

Active in community affairs, she is a founding member of the Dallas County R-1 Alumni Association and has served on the board since its organization in 1971. She is an associate member of American Mothers, Inc.

Writing is her passion but home, family, business, and community activities claim priority. In her world, *Every Day Is Mother's Day.*

To Mother with Love:

Until the day she died, my mother was never old, to me. She was the young, beautiful, vibrant woman who saved rationed gasoline, put my two younger brothers and me into a war-weary car, and drove through the nights on thin tires to follow my father from army base to army base before he went overseas.

> Robert Vaughan
> Author of *Touch the Face of God*

My mom was the world's best mom. She was pure love personified. I can only aspire to be as wonderful as she was.

> Bobbie Smith
> *New York Times* best-selling author, wife, mother, and
> grandmother

Mom saw more in me than I saw in myself. She always listened carefully and encouraged the positive step forward.

> Jack C. Shewmaker
> Retired President and Vice Chairman,
> Wal-Mart Stores, Inc.

My mother . . . has eleven children. Anything I have accomplished would pale in comparison to her achievements.

> Len Dawson
> Former professional football player
> Presently award winning sport anchor for KMBC 9 News,
> Kansas City

One of the ways I like to remember my mother is the way she looked in those old sepia-toned pictures I used to study in our family albums. She was this beautiful, athletic teenager who, before turning 16, could swim all the way across Lake Howard and had read every book in the Winter Haven (Florida) library. Her laugh was infectious, and my wife says that I got my comedic timing from her, Margaret Garland Stafford. Her name was graceful – like she was. As you can tell, I adored her.

Jim Stafford

Jim Stafford's unique talents, wry sense of humor, and incredible guitar pickin' made him a multi-faceted entertainer and international entertainment personality. His wit, charm, and natural ease make him an adept host and star performer at his Branson, Missouri, theater.

"Mom, travel with me on this tour. I know you've been to Morocco but you've always wanted to go to Japan. After Morocco, we'll travel to London and back to Japan."

Payne Stewart (to his mother)
Legend in the world of PGA golf

Unforgettable memories remain traveling together with Payne on his golf tours. William Payne Stewart, a combination of his father's name and mine, was the way he signed his name when he entered a tournament.

Bee Payne-Stewart
Mother to the late William Payne Stewart